"EXTERMINATE THEM"

"EXTERMINATE THEM"

Written Accounts of the Murder, Rape, and Slavery
of Native Americans During the California Gold
Rush, 1848–1868

Edited by
Clifford E. Trafzer
and
Joel R. Hyer

Michigan State University Press

East Lansing

∞ The paper used in this publication meets the minimum requirements of
ANSI/NISO Z39.48–1992 (R 1997) (Permanence of Paper).

Michigan State University Press
East Lansing, Michigan 48823-5202

03 02 01 00 99   1 2 3 4 5 6

Library of Congress Cataloging-in-Publication Data

Trafzer, Clifford E.
    Exterminate them : written accounts of the murder, rape, and slavery of Native
Americans during the California gold rush, 1848–1868 / by Clifford E. Trafzer and
Joel R. Hyer. ·
    p.   cm.
    Includes bibliographical references and index.
    ISBN 0-87013-501-5
    1. Indians, Treatment of—California—History. 2. Indians, Treatment of—
California—History—Sources. 3. Indians of North America—Crimes against—
California. 4. California—Gold discoveries—Social aspects. I. Hyer, Joel R. II.
Title.
E78.C15175 1999   98-51988
323.1'1970794'09034—dc21   CIP

Cover design by Heidi Dailey
Book design by Michael J. Brooks

Visit Michigan State University Press on the World-Wide Web
    http://www.msu.edu/unit/msupress

We respectfully dedicate this work to Ashlee and Joshua Joel and to our friends and colleagues among California's Indian people.

Katherine Saubel
Dean Mike
Karlene Vernaci
Larry Myers
William Mungary
Dorothy Joseph
Edward Castillo
Patricia Dixon
Lorena Dixon
Ron Christman
Virginia Christman
Anthony Madrigal
Luke Madrigal
Jane Dumas
Rupert Costo
Jayne Liera
Temet Aguilar
Darryl Babe Wilson
Jack Norton
Dalbert Castro
Henry Rodriquez
David Lucero
Marc Macarro
Joe Benitez

This publication was made possible in part from research funds provided by the Costo Historical and Linguistics Native American Research Center and Publications in Native American Studies, University of California, Riverside.

CONTENTS

FOREWORD

In the early winter of 1848, Johann August Sutter, a former Mexican governmental official, local *caudillo* (warlord), and Indian slave owner, hastily convened a meeting with the chief of the Colma Nissenan Indians. Appointed by the military governor as the new United States Indian subagent and now apparently a rehabilitated ex-Mexican Patriot, Sutter shouldered the task of establishing official relations with the local tribesmen that he had until recently terrorized and enslaved. His first order of business was to negotiate a "treaty" with Coloma tribesmen that would lease the entire watershed of the American River to Sutter personally. After all, gold had recently been discovered at a sawmill he had commissioned to be constructed nearby. During the negotiations, Sutter was warned by the chief that the yellow metal he so eagerly sought "belonged to a demon who devoured all who searched for it." In a moment of clarity, the military governor of Alta California denied Sutter's self-serving actions. Nevertheless, the chief's dire predictions proved to be devastatingly on target.

In popular literature and school textbooks the events that followed the discovery of gold have for too long been portrayed as a great adventure, luring American males to the far west in search of personal fortunes and validating the hysterically popular doctrine of Manifest Destiny. The predominate theme in these representations has been the personal sacrifices, hardships, and ultimate disappointment in the great enterprise. The fate of the California Indians was, like Indian futures everywhere, doomed and dismissed into the waste bin of history. After all, these writers reasoned, the Indians were a stone-age people who, in social Darwinistic dogma, must inevitably yield to the overpowering force of a technologically "superior people." This book is about the human cost of that adventure.

ix

Underlying the events chronicled in this documented history of the California Indians in the gold rush is what I describe as the "chaos theory" of Gold Rush history. Historians and other writers have the tendency to assemble historical documents and measurable facts in such a way as to construct a rational, modular organization of data chronicling events that seem to unfold in a rather pedestrian and predictable manner. Studies of gold rush mining laws, the adoption of the state constitution in 1850, and other historical facts seem to suggest an orderly and ultimately responsible reaction to the hectic events of a nineteenth-century mining frontier. However, a more analytical, thoughtful and critical study of this era through its historical documents reveals quite the contrary. There was, in fact, a complete breakdown of all legal and moral constraints on American immigrants' civic and criminal behavior. For example, California's first governor bluntly advocated Indian genocide by declaring, "A war of extermination will continue to be waged between the races until the Indian race becomes extinct."

This work documents the creation of state laws that virtually enslaved California Indians, despite the fact that California entered the Union as a "free" state. It further reveals the systematic abrogation of guarantees of protection for Indian land and civil rights according to the Treaty of Guadalupe Hidalgo. This international agreement had severed Mexico's tenuous hold on the population and territory of Alta California. The state constitutional convention deemed Indian citizenship, property, and civil rights and their right to testify in court proceedings to be unimportant. Consequently the state's native peoples were relegated to the legal status of extraconstitutional nonpersons. This legal chicanery made possible the greatest orgy of land fraud, dispossession, slavery, and mass murder ever witnessed in North American Indian history. The period from 1850 to 1868 was essentially a twisted Darwinian laboratory showcasing the triumph of brute force aided by a pathogenic and technological assault on a native people unparalleled in Western hemispheric history.

In fact nothing even remotely similar to the mass murder and concomitant, gut-wrenching vortex of population decline seen in this period has ever been recorded in United States history. This is not to dismiss the traumatic removal, aggressive military assaults, and dispossession of Cherokees during the 1828 Georgia Gold Rush in their beloved homeland. Nor does it trivialize the devastating effects of the 1876 Black Hills gold discovery in the sacred Black Hills of the Dakotas. Even the Alaskan Gold Rush at the turn of this century fails to provide a comparable example of territorial loss or a comparable body count.

As the 150th anniversary of the California gold discovery approached, I, along with many other California Indians, struggled with my conscious about how I might participate in the California Sesquicentennial in an honest and dignified manner. To ignore it would be to surrender to those who would trivialize the violent annihilation of something like half of our surviving population. For those interested in only the bottom line, 100,000 California Indians died in the first two years of the Gold Rush. Not much here to celebrate.

Wyandot Indian historian Professor Cliff Trafzer and his coauthor Joel Hyer have assembled a collection of documents that bear stark testimony to the heartless and methodical manner in which the aboriginal population of California was systematically dispossessed of its homeland and routinely oppressed, exploited, and terrorized.

Many of the documents and newspaper accounts found in this volume have been previously published. Unfortunately many of those publications are now out of print and frequently are difficult to find.

In the early 1970s I pursued a graduate program in American anthropology with the esteemed scholar Robert F. Heizer. He published many of these documents in a number of limited editions. What distinguishes this study from Heizer's early document anthologies is the inclusion of contextual historical and ethnographic background information. Despite these considerations, all contemporary California history scholars and students, and other seekers of historical truths, are indebted to Heizer and his many California Indian informants.

In contrast, this work presents a comprehensive and focused look at historical data and an assessment of the impact of the Gold Rush on the Indians of California. In the following pages the reader will find an eye-opening and disturbing glimpse of the colonization of the golden state and the Indian response to it. This is a very important text and will provide today's readers with contemporary Gold Rush civilian and military accounts.

Only an honest and frank discussion of the legacy of the Gold Rush can provide today's Californians and others with a balanced understanding of this state's defining event. It is no small irony that the present state executive is determined that Indian gaming be dominated and controlled by the "compassionate" government that declared its intention to destroy Indians in a genocidal struggle little more than a century and a half ago.

History is often painful and disturbing, but it is always enlightening.

Edward D. Castillo
A Cahuilla Man

PREFACE

G old and Gold Rush! The words bring forth romantic images of sourdough miners clad in bright flannel shirts, wearing worn-out Levis, scuffed boots, and floppy felt hats. Bending over the rocky shore of roaring rivers, these white miners pannned for gold with the diligence and perseverance that made America what it is today. American history texts, particularly those designed for young readers, are filled with positive images glorifying the Forty-Niners and the California Gold Rush. The Gold Rush in California is part of the "Mining Frontier" that opened the American West to white civilization, economic development, social advancement, and statehood. What is generally missing from these accounts are California's Indians and the holocaust brought by miners to the First Nations of California.

California's Indians survived the holocaust, but they are not celebrating the Sesquicentennial of the gold discovery at Coloma in 1848. They are lamenting the rape, murder, and enslavement of their people that began with the discovery of gold by Indians and whites at Sutter's Mill on the American River. Native Americans throughout California are remembering that white miners murdered thousands of Indians, raped hundreds of native women and children, and sold thousands of people into slavery. Population figures vary depending on the source, but scholars generally feel that in 1846 the California Indian population was at least 120,000—if not more—but had plummeted by the 1860s to somewhere between 20,000 and 40,000. The most dramatic era of population reduction came between 1848 and 1868, when approximately 100,000 Indians died from disease, malnutrition, enslavement, and murder. In spite of the continued decline of the native population to roughly 17,000 in 1900, California's Indian population has recovered and survived.

Hupa scholar Jack Norton and anthropologist Florence Shipek argue that the precontact population of California was as high as one million and that the Indian population in 1846 was likely higher than 120,000. But the native people who were murdered, raped, and enslaved in California are not numbers or statistics to be debated by scholars. They were human beings, members of families, and loved ones. The rapes, murders, kidnappings, and enslavements came at a horrendous cost to California's first peoples. Within a matter of a few years, the people lost their parents and grandparents, sisters and brothers, sons and daughters. They lost the providers for their villages, the spiritual leaders, the tribal historians, and the leadership for future generations. The people lost their land and resources, but worst of all, they lost their security and much of their hope. People fell into a state of despair, depression, and anomie. Native peoples in California suffered from tremendous trauma that still affects them.

Since the days of the Gold Rush California's Indians have mourned, and mourning continues during the state's celebration of the great events of the 1840s and 1850s. Every tribe and village remembers the Gold Rush and the white atrocities of the era. Scholars such as Jack Norton have collected oral histories of the Gold Rush among contemporary Indians. The following presentation offers another source of information, one written by whites themselves about the Gold Rush era. The newspapers of California during the 1840s to the 1860s, particularly the leading paper, the *Daily Alta California*, provide one window into the holocaust suffered by California's Indians during the Gold Rush. Most of the murders, rapes, and enslavements occurred in Northern California, where the newspaper was headquartered. But the articles run by the *Daily Alta California* often appeared in other newspapers around the state and beyond. Many of the entries found in this volume are from the *Daily Alta California*, but other newspapers are also included, particularly if they presented local and regional news about the killing fields of California.

In addition, we have included a few choice letters and some information on the California state law that discriminated against Indians, establishing an indentured system (legalized slavery) among California Indians and establishing the right of whites to control Indian children. From the 1850s to the 1880s, the state had greater influence over Indian affairs in California than did the federal government, and state and local officials used their power to dispossess the First Nations of their estates and birthrights. Local sheriffs and justices of the peace allowed non-Indians to steal Indian lands and resources. In their pathbreaking works, Robert Heizer, Alan Almquist, Sherburne Cook, Edward Castillo, James Rawls, George Phillips, Florence Shipek, and Richard

Carrico disclose some of these abuses and document specific incidences of murders, rapes, and enslavement. However, although some scholars know of this body of work, others ignore it. In 1997, for example, Malcolm Rohrbough published *Days of Gold* with the University of California Press, but his presentation barely mentions Indians and does not discuss the holocaust among California's Indians.

Robert F. Heizer and Alan Almquist published *The Other Californians* in 1971, and Heizer published *They Were Only Diggers* and *The Destruction of California Indians* three years later. These volumes detailed elements of the murders, rapes, slavery, and discrimination perpetrated against California's Indians, but unfortunately their works did not greatly influence the way American history was written about the era. James Rawls's book of 1984, *Indians of California*, has made some impact, but still most historians, educators, and public officials are unaware of the California Indian holocaust. Perhaps this work will add to the growing number of sources that deconstruct a destructive time in the nation's past. It may encourage scholars, teachers, politicians, and the general public to reexamine California's past and the glorious image of the gold miners and whites who stole California and resettled land that had belonged to California's original people since the beginning of time. Teachers may find the newspaper articles helpful in their classroom presentation, while scholars may wish to use the accounts to enrich their presentations of the Gold Rush era.

The volume is primarily a compilation of original newspaper accounts from newspapers of the 1840s-60s. We used microfilm copies of most newspapers cited in the work, but in a few cases we used hard copies of the newspapers. Whenever we did not use the original source, we noted our source for the article. There are several versions of some articles, depending on which newspaper ran the article, since many of the newpapers ran articles that had previously appeared in other newspapers. Some of the articles were edited or abbreviated, but each article that appears in this book is exactly as it appeared in the sources cited.

Several people and institutions have helped us create this work. We are indebted to Sapna Patel who helped present the final draft of this manuscript. Her careful work has added greatly to the organization and presentation of this book, and we are grateful. We thank our British colleagues, Ian Chambers and Waughnita Goins, for finding key articles in their original form and Richard Hanks, who shared his research from the scrapbooks of Judge Benjamin Hayes. We appreciate the cooperation given to us by the librarians at the Bancroft Library, Huntington Library, San Diego State University Library, and the libraries at the University of California, Riverside, and the

University of California, Los Angeles. Without the help and cooperation of many people and institutions, this work could not have been completed.

Several scholars have helped us in our work by commenting on various aspects of the work or reading portions of the manuscript. We wish to thank Edward Castillo, Director of Native American Studies at Sonoma State University; Donna Akers, Director of American Indian Studies at California State University, Northridge; Duane Champagne, Director of the American Indian Center at the University of California, Los Angeles; Troy Johnson of California State University, Long Beach; James Sandos, Farquar Professor of the Southwest at the University of Redlands; James Rawls, Professor of History at Diablo Valley College; and Monte Kugel, Professor of History at the University of California, Riverside.

We extend a special thanks to Carlos Velez-Ibañez, Max Neiman, Carl Crannor, Sharon Salinger, and David Warren, who have been so supportive of our research. Our colleagues in the Department of History and Ethnic Studies, particularly Armando Navarro, Steffi San Buenaventura, and Sterling Stuckey, have also helped us with our work in many ways. Maria Anna Gonzales of the Social Science Research Center has been instrumental in this work, and we thank her sincerely for all of her work. We thank Dean and Theresa Mike as well as other Chemehuevis of the Twenty-Nine Palms Band of Mission Indians for their interest and support. Luke and Anthony Madrigal, Jack Norton, and Florence Shipek kindly shared their research and helped us improve this work. We dedicate our work to several people, including a few California Indians who have influenced our lives. Finally, we thank Lee Ann, Tess, Hayley, and Tara, as well as Ashlee and Joshua, for their understanding and support as we worked to introduce and edit this book.

Clifford E. Trafzer, Yucaipa, California
Joel R. Hyer, Riverside, California
January 1999

INTRODUCTION

Holocaust is an excellent word to use to describe the terror, death, and destruction brought to Native Americans in California during the era of the Gold Rush. One might also use the words extermination, debasement, or genocide to depict Indian-white relations from 1848–68. The *Chico Courant* of July 28, 1866 offered the position that "It is a mercy to the red devils to exterminate them, and a saving of many white lives Treaties are played out—there is one kind of treaty that is effective—cold lead."[1] This was a point of view expressed by other editors in California, one that resonates throughout California's dark and hidden past—one that does not appear in popular literature of the Gold Rush era. This was not the view of all non-Indians of California, but one that helped stir a bloody killing field in California and cost the native population thousands of lives.

It had not started out that way. In 1848 a group of Maidu, Nissinan, and other California Indians joined James Marshall in his task to build a saw mill on the American River for John Sutter. Indians led Marshall to a Maidu village called Coloma where the white man decided to build the mill. In order for the mill to operate, Marshall ordered his Indian employees to dig a mill race. Native California Indians dug the mill race and found gold nuggets in the process, showing them to whites, including James Marshall. The Indians had lived in the foothills of the Sierra Nevada Mountains for generations, and they had seen gold before. However, they placed no value on the metal. But the gold found on January 24, 1848 had great meaning to the white men working at Coloma, and the gold discovery would have significant meaning to thousands of California Indians and peoples throughout the world.[2]

When the Gold Rush began in 1848, Californios who ran extensive ranches in California packed up their Indian cowboys, Indian families, and

1

took them to the streams rushing through the Foothills of the Sierra Nevada Mountains. Approximately 4,000 Indian miners worked in the gold fields by 1850, and in 1848, Acting Governor Richard B. Mason reported that over half the miners in California were Indians.[3] However, this quickly changed after white miners from Oregon began murdering Indian miners, and it became unhealthy for most Indians to remain the in the gold fields. White men coming to California resented the Californios, in part because some of them were of Spanish and Mexican ancestry, but more importantly because white miners felt that the Californios had an unfair advantage by using large numbers of Indian miners. Many whites hated Indians, and some of them organized vigilante or militia groups to prevent Californios and Indians from taking too much gold. Their solution was to harass Indian miners, burn their villages, or kill them outright. This had been a successful technique in dealing with Indians used by the Spanish, English, French, Russian, and other European invaders, and it was employed successfully by white miners in California.

In his account, *An Excursion to California*, British Forty-Niner William Kelly wrote in 1851 that a storekeeper in the gold fields told him that "no Christian man is bound to give full value to those infernal red-skins" since California's Indians were "vagabones and have no more bissness with money than a mule or a wolf." The storekeeper added that Indians have "no religion, and tharfore no consciences."[4] Like the storekeepers, other whites did not consider California Indians to be human, calling them "Diggers," a pejorative term related to the better-known term, "Nigger." In addition to cheating Indians, white miners began raping and murdering Indians in March, 1849 when Oregon miners raped Maidu Indian women at a village along the American River. When Maidu men tried to rescue their daughters, sisters, and wives, the Oregonians shot them to death. Oregonian countered with an attack on an Indian village on Weber's Creek, killing twelve or more Indians and capturing many more. The Oregonians took seven or eight of these Indian captives to Coloma where the whites told them to run. When they did, the white men shot them to death. The great killings of California's first people had begun.[5]

Bloodshed along the American River was not the first spilled in California, but the event foreshadowed future events of greater severity and magnitude. A year after Indians had found gold at Coloma, roving bands of armed men murdered men, women, and children in a war to destroy all obstacles in the way of native land, water, and mineral resources. White men murdered Indians in a defensive war in order to kill native peoples before Indians could kill them. Miners literally drove Indians from their native lands, stealing their resources and claiming land that had been the homes of native peoples for

generations. Many miners were young men raised in the United States during the 1820s and 1830s, and they had lived through the forced removal of
thousands of Indians from every corner of the eastern United States. White
farmers, merchants, and militia forces had driven Wyandots, Shawnees,
Lenape, Ottawa, Anishinaabe, and others from Ohio, Cherokees from
Tennessee and Georgia, Choctaws from Mississippi, and Muscogees from
Alabama. White miners recreated the violence of their fathers and grandfa-
thers, making Native Californians "strangers in a stolen land."[6]

NATIVE CALIFORNIA INDIANS

Circumstances surrounding the California Indian holocaust did not begin in
a vacuum. By 1848 and the birth of the Gold Rush era, California's Indians
had witnessed many changes as a result of their contact with Spaniards,
Russians, Mexicans, and other Euro-Americans. Prior to European contact,
Native Americans had dwelled for centuries in what is now California. The
relatively mild climate, coupled with abundant resources, enabled the diverse,
indigenous populations to flourish. In California, native peoples resided in
arid deserts, rich valleys, rolling foothills, rugged mountains, and along the
Pacific coast. Depending on their location, Native Californians subsisted on
an abundance of food resources, including fish, deer, rabbit, and shellfish.[7]

Most California Indians relied on acorns as a staple food, and the entire
region was rich in natural foods. Women typically ground acorn meal into a
flour, drenched it with water to remove the unpalatable tannic acid, and
baked it into flat bread or used it to make mush or pudding. They ate a diet
rich in natural fruits, vegetables, seeds, and nuts as well as meat, fowl, and
fish. All of these foods contributed greatly to the well-being of California's
first people, for over the centuries they had developed a biological reliance on
them. Beginning with the Spanish period and continuing through the
American period, natural habitats for fish, game, and plants foods declined
due to ranching, agriculture, and other economic development. The Gold
Rush brought white miners who summarily destroyed natural habitats,
killing plants and animals while introducing more livestock and alien plants
that destroyed the natural landscape of California. In addition to the outright
murder of Indians during the era of the Gold Rush, Indians lost their native
foods for which they had a biological and spiritual relationship. The destruction of this relationship further jeopardized the lives of native peoples.

By 1769, at least 300,000 Indians lived in California, although this number
provided by Alfred Kroeber is believed by contemporary scholars to have
been a low estimate. California's Indians speaking over one hundred distinct

languages. Instead of belonging to "tribes," these Native Americans dwelled in smaller groups, including bands and villages that were often autonomous but culturally and linguistically related to their neighbors. Frequent contact among these native peoples resulted in extensive trade networks. Coastal and interior groups conducted trade with each other, often traveling great distances to exchange baskets, beads, shells, herbs, and seeds. Many tribes also traded with peoples living in Mexico, the Southwest, Great Basin, Northwest Coast, and Northwest Plateau. Indeed, oral traditions among Native Californians indicate that they had a relationship with Native Hawai'ians and other peoples of the Pacific Islands.[8]

While some Indians forged relatively peaceful relations with each other, others were more inclined to warfare. The contemporary image of California's Indians—created by the Catholic Church and its historians— is one of native peoples always being "docile and domesticated." This is an unfounded image born of the mission system where Indians were and are depicted as kneeling neophytes accepting of the Christian dogma brought by the Franciscans without question or intelligence. Violent confrontations often erupted among Native Californians, stemming from competition over natural resources as well as hunting grounds. Other conflicts arose between old enemies or competing leaders, and some of these animosities continued for generations. Despite this, boundaries between "tribes" appear to have remained fairly stable, although it is clear that some groups expanded onto lands previously controlled by a former group.

In spite of conflicts, American Indians in California developed rich cultures that have endured for generations. Because of the mild climate and abundance of foods, native peoples developed complex religions, social systems, laws, literature, economies, and arts. Dance, music and song flourished in California and continues to grow today. Many Native Californians were known for their beautiful basketry, an art form that has been revitalized by native weavers and is growing rapidly today. Numerous peoples of California excelled in the art of basket weaving and developed elaborate religious ceremonies, festivals, and oral traditions that required the use and remembrance of basketry. Ajumawe and Atsugewe scholar Darryl Babe Wilson has pointed out that the people of the Pit River country believe that at the time of creation, a basket was placed into the peak of Mount Shasta where it remains today sending out its contents of peace and good will. Baskets are more than material culture and art objects. They are spiritual elements of the communities woven into the history, culture, and religion of the peoples.[9]

SPAIN'S INVASION

Spanish invasions into the region eventually altered the world of many California Indians. During the first half of the sixteenth century, Spaniards explored vast regions of the Americas in search of gold and other precious metals. In 1540, Francisco Vasquez de Coronado penetrated what is now the American Southwest, while his associates Hernan de Alarcon and Melchior Diaz briefly entered Alta and Baja California. Two years later, Juan Rodriguez Cabrillo and his men sailed up the California coast, making contact with Kumeyaays living near the shores of San Diego Bay and Tongva-Chumash of Catalina Island. Subsequent voyages up the coast by Sir Francis Drake and Sebastian Vizcaíno also resulted in minor interaction between Europeans and Indians. By right of discovery, these Europeans' nations claimed California, and Spain proclaimed that California's native peoples were subjects of the crown. Spain claimed Alta California but did not resettle the region until 1769.[10]

Despite these encounters, the Spanish did not invade and conquer California until they had heard rumors of Russian vessels sailing along the California coast during the 1760s. José de Gálvez, the *visitador-general* of New Spain, feared the Russian presence on the northern frontier of the Spanish Empire. In order to fortify that region from Russian control, Gálvez dispatched a major expedition in 1769 led by Gaspar de Portolá and Father Junípero Serra. The priest set out to establish Catholic missions throughout upper California and convert the Indians to Christianity. He brought religious materials to achieve those ends as well as seeds and vegetables to instruct the Native Americans regarding European agricultural methods. Although Serra and other priests may have possessed what they considered to be honorable intentions in converting the Indians to Christianity, their presence introduced devastating diseases, widespread despair, and genocide among California's native peoples. [11]

Experiences prior to the conquest of California profoundly influenced Spanish attitudes toward non-Europeans. In 711, Muslims from North Africa crossed the Strait of Gibraltar and seized much of the Iberian Peninsula. Between 718 and 1492, the people who would become the Spanish and Portuguese gradually reconquered the Iberian Peninsula. During these centuries—in what Spaniards regarded to be a series of holy wars—Spain regained lost territories, became increasingly militant, and developed a vicious form of racism. According to the Spanish, Europeans were Christian, white, upright, civilized, and crusaders for God's holy causes. They contended that their victories against the Muslims confirmed their superiority.

In contrast, they considered non-Europeans to be savage, dark, idolatrous, and uncivilized. Spaniards carried these notions to the Americas and treated indigenous inhabitants with deadly severity.

In California, as well as in other parts of the Spanish Empire, Spaniards endeavored to make Native Americans into productive Spanish citizens and Christians. However, Spaniards never intended for California's Indian people to be equals to Spaniards born in Spain or Mexico. They were not even to be equals with mestizos. California's Indians were seen as a labor force within and outside of the mission system. They were to be the laborers who would allow Spain to reshape California into a bulwark against intrusion by other European powers. Spain sought to accomplish this by founding missions, presidios, and pueblos. These three institutions set in motion Indian cultural decline and resulted in the physical demise of at least one hundred thousand California Native Americans—perhaps more.

Beginning in 1769 when Father Serra began Mission San Diego, the system ultimately included twenty-one missions. The missions stretched from San Diego to Sonoma, stretching along El Camino Real—the King's Highway—which ran along or near the west coast of California. Serra and his missionaries created reducciones or reductions where Catholic priests worked to destroy native culture and religion, replacing it with Christianity. Some priests sincerely desired to save the souls of native peoples and win their allegiance. Clearly, some missionaries viewed proselytization of California's native inhabitants as a labor of love, but many—including Father Serra—employed brutality and intimidation to achieve their goals. They attempted to entice Indians with food and European goods in order to lure them into the missions. When this failed, the padres solicited the aid of Spanish soldiers, who captured Native Americans and forced them to remain within the Catholic missions. [12]

Forced concentration and imprisonment of Native Californians within the mission system is an element of the mission's history that the Church fails to share in its contemporary presentations of these historic sites. The Church also denies whipping men, women, and children, actually characterizing the beatings as "spankings." Spanish soldiers and Christian neophytes ran down Indians who escaped imprisonment at the missions, forcing families to remain within the mission system in violation of the teachings of Jesus. The missions served as reduction centers where Spanish priests, with military support, attempted to reduce Native American peoples and cultures and rebuild them through Catholic discipline. Spanish soldiers concentrated various indigenous peoples into one village in an attempt to destroy the link of the people to each other and their villages. The Catholic fathers then commenced the so-called "civilization" process. They baptized entire villages en mass, forced Spanish law and Christian dogma on the people, and diligently tried to destroy their native languages by requiring Spanish to be spoken.

The Church also forced California's Indians to do nearly all of the work in the missions and labor as slaves of Christ. Native men, women, and children mixed mud for adobes, built forms for adobe blocks, hauled the mud and bricks, laid the bricks, cut timbers for vigas, and made tiles for the structures. Native Californians became cobblers, carpenters, masons. Indians cleared fields for orchards and crops. They planted, harvested, and preserved foods in the missions. They learned to ride horses so they could herd the longhorn cattle brought by the Spaniards, and they slaughtered cattle so they could make tallow to help finance the missions. Christian missionaries exploited Indian labor, and as the missions became economic institutions, priests demanded that their laborers remain within the mission system so they could work, become civilized, and be converted fully to the one true religion. Native religious leaders and their doctrines were obstacles to the missionaries who sought to root out and destroy these elements of California Indian culture. Native Americans encountered miserable conditions in the missions. Perceiving Indians to be children, priests humiliated, flogged, and incarcerated them for various offenses. [13]

Some missionaries reportedly wanted to turn the missions over to the Indians within ten years, yet this never happened. Instead, Catholic fathers subjected Indians to forced labor, poor living conditions, and rampant diseases that mercilessly took the lives of tens of thousands of Native Americans. For the indigenous peoples of California, the mission system was a living nightmare, and memories of native life within the missions remains a haunting memory to many California Indians—Christians and non-Christians. However, the mission was not the only institution of the Spanish Empire that affected Indians. Presidios and pueblos also constituted vital elements of Spain's plans to make the Indians of California loyal subjects.

Most presidios or Spanish forts served to support the missions, although they were separate institutions under a different bureaucracy than the Church. The four military installations in California—located in San Francisco, Monterey, Santa Barbara, and San Diego—housed soldiers who searched for runaway Indians and protected the missions from attack. Spanish and Indian accounts both attest to the fact that soldiers frequently raped native women and indiscriminately murdered native men for protesting the rape of their daughters, wives, mothers, and grandmothers. Soldiers summarily murdered Indians for protecting their families. Sexual abuses were so grave at Mission San Diego that Father Luis Jayme asked Serra to permit him to move Mission San Diego up the San Diego River, a request that Serra granted.[14]

Pueblos built by Spaniards from New Spain, provided village communities for Spaniards, including the families of soldiers. Officials in New Spain encouraged Spaniards to move to California by promising them "free" land, real estate that rightfully was controlled by Indians but claimed by the Spaniards by right of discovery and right of conquest. Spanish farmers at the pueblos sold surplus crops to presidios and fought Indians in emergencies. In other words, Spaniards living at the pueblos upheld and strengthened the presidios and missions which sought to alter the lives and destroy the cultures of California's native peoples. In addition, pueblos served as examples for Indians so that they could witness a "civilized" life. The increasing presence of Spanish immigrants had disastrous consequences for the Indians and their environment.

Spaniards who resettled California, displacing the native population, introduced sheep, horses, mules, and cattle which overgrazed lands. Alien livestock consumed vast quantities of grasses and other plants, driving away native game and making hunting for traditional game more difficult. Livestock also destroyed plant habitats of natural foods that were critical to Native Californians. Thus, the Spanish incursion into California disrupted the delicate balance which existed between Indian peoples and the earth, plants, and animals. However, as dramatic as these changes were to native peoples, they could not compare to those that emerged with the invasion of the United States and discovery of gold at Coloma. [15]

CALIFORNIA INDIAN AGENCY AND RESISTANCE

Despite the Spanish systems of coercion, Indians resisted foreign domination, sometimes subtly, other times violently. In the missions, Native Americans occasionally disregarded orders or instructions given by the priests. Although Indians learned the Spanish language and various tenets of Catholicism, they frequently retained their native languages, religious beliefs, rituals, ceremonies, songs, and oral narratives. Young Native American men defied the strict gender-segregated living conditions at the missions slipping into the monjarios or dormitories of young Indian women. Sometimes women escaped their nightly imprisonment to be with friends and families they loved. Native women defied the Church by aborting babies conceived by being raped by soldiers, civil officials, or priests.

Hundreds of Native California Indians expressed their disdain for the missions by fleeing into the interior of California. Patriots among the native people who fled the missions often confiscated Spanish weapons and horses.

When they returned to their people or joined other groups of Indians, they often gave riding lessons and taught military tactics to those Indians not under Spanish control. These Indians became raiders and forces that harassed the Spanish throughout the mission period. Thousands of Native Americans abhorred the Spanish presence and struggled to expel them from the region. For instance, approximately eight hundred Kumeyaay Indians (also known as Ipai and Tipai), representing perhaps three dozen villages or more, stormed the San Diego Mission and burned it to the ground in 1775. Father Jayme had built the new mission in the heart of Nipaguay, a Kumeyaay village that was unearthed in 1989–90 when the Diocese attempt to build a fellowship hall and bingo parlor on top of the mission, village, and Indian cemetery. [16]

Kumeyaay leaders—particularly religious leaders—who encouraged, planned, organized, and executed the action against Mission San Diego viewed Christianity as a threat to their traditional culture. This was no less true of other California Indians. In 1781, Quechans living along the Colorado River attacked two nearby pueblos at Mission La Purisima de la Concepcíon and Mission San Palbo y San Pedro de Bicuity as a threat to their traditional culture. This was no less true of other California Indians. In 1781, a Spanish army under Pedro Fages rescued the captives, the Spanish never returned to resettle the region or challenge Quechan rule of their homelands. In fact, Quechans successfully harassed Spanish and Mexican herders and immigrants traveling to California, thereby curtailing further settlement. [17]

Other less successful uprisings occurred at numerous locations, including Mission San Gabriel in 1785–86, Missions Santa Clara and San Juan Bautista between 1790 and 1800, and the Mission Santa Cruz in 1812. The most spectacular example of resistance among the Native Americans of California occurred in 1824, three years after Mexico's independence from Spain. Between 1772 and 1804, Spanish overlords forced Chumash Indians inhabiting the coast between Los Angeles and San Luis Obispo to participate in the construction of five missions and one presidio on native lands. Many of this people had suffered ill treatment by local Spanish soldiers and priests. In February 1824, the Spanish had an Indian at San Ynez Mission flogged, and the event resulted in a massive native revolt. Indians living at the mission rose up and attacked their oppressors and destroyed several structures. The next day, almost two thousand Native Americans seized and fortified the nearby La Purísima Concepcíon Mission. Chumash Indians from the missions at San Ynez and San Fernando soon traveled to La Purísima to reinforce that mission against the Spanish. [18]

News regarding these events reached the Santa Barbara Mission not long afterward. Tensions rose there. Fearing that the Indians might rebel, Spanish soldiers—without provocation from local native people—attacked Indian laborers at Santa Barbara. After fighting several hours, the Spanish withdrew from the mission. The Native American victors then destroyed the mission and retired to safer territory. One month after these initial takeovers, Spanish soldiers mounted an attack on Mission de la Purísima. Padres eventually negotiated a cease-fire between the two parties. While most of the Chumash Indians received little or no punishment for participating in these events, the Spanish condemned and executed seven of their leaders for their involvement in the uprisings. The Spanish viewed the conflict as a revolution against their regime, but contemporary Chumash argue that they acted as patriots against foreign invaders who had stolen their lands, oppressed their people, and forced many cultural changes.

Mexico's Rule

The years between 1821 and 1846 marked the period of Mexican rule in California. The new nation of Mexico inherited a massive, overextended empire from Spain. Mexicans assumed control over the missions, presidios, and pueblos of Baja and Alta California. As demonstrated by the Chumash fight for freedom, Native Americans at the missions resisted the priests throughout the Spanish colonial era in a variety of ways. In 1821, over twenty-one thousand Indians resided and worked at the missions. Widespread disease, death, and the escaping of Indians reduced that number to sixteen thousand by 1834. Missionaries hoped to force additional laborers from outlying native villages and establish a series of new missions into the interior. Yet the dearth of money and personnel prevented the fruition of these plans. Instead of growing, the mission system declined rapidly during the Mexican era of California's native past.

In 1833, the government of Mexico passed legislation secularizing the missions of California. The new laws stipulated that local officials were to distribute mission lands to native peoples who had converted to Catholicism. These Indians were to receive half of the missions' livestock, seeds, and tools. Instead of complying with the statutes, civil authorities confiscated most of the mission lands for themselves, forcefully pushing California's Indians aside and denying them lands that had belonged to them since the time of their creation. On extensive, prime, mission lands, Mexican officials and wealthy landowners established large, private ranchos, stealing former mission lands that had been intended—under law—to be returned to the native population. Rather than regaining their traditional lands, California's native population became the labor force for the ranchos. Many of California's Indians became vaqueros, cooks, wranglers, and general employees—the labor force—for Californio rancheros.[19]

These changing conditions offered new choices for indigenous inhabitants of California. They could work on the ranchos or in one of the developing Mexican towns, doing wage labor. They could apply for their own land grants, although this was an avenue rarely pursued by First Nation's people in California. Or, native people in California could move away from the Mexican population and join their friends and relatives, forming new and dynamic social, political, and economic units. Some Indians worked in towns such as Los Angeles, San Diego, San José, San Francisco, and Santa Cruz. Many of these communities became completely dependent upon native labor, as Indians and non-Indians interacted with each other on a constant and daily level in such occupations as smiths, cobblers, wheelwrights, whalers, and teamsters. Indians labored in fields near Los Angeles and San José, harvesting grapes and other crops. Native Americans worked on ranchos, performing numerous tasks, including shearing sheep, raising crops, herding and slaughtering cattle, dressing hides, and building houses. Californio rancheros did not generally regulate the noneconomic affairs of native laborers, but largely ignored native religious ceremonies, music, art, and festivals. Throughout the Spanish and Mexican periods, native peoples nurtured and preserved various aspects of their diverse cultures, and Californios made no concerted effort to destroy native religions, rituals, or ceremonies.

A few Indians filed for Mexican land grants in California, but most did not, and their "legal" title to their homes has been a major issue ever since the eighteenth century. The process of filing a land grant included written documents, legal processes, and paper work, Indians who succeeded in this endeavor tended to be literate and knowledgeable about Mexican law. Through these means, a few Native Americans eventually possessed ranchos two thousand acres in size. Such men appear to have led lifestyles more like local Mexican rancheros than their indigenous predecessors. Indian women also asserted themselves in this manner. In 1838, one native woman named Victoria obtained a rancho in the San Gabriel Valley. By 1852, at least fifty Native Americans had secured "legal" land titles in southern California alone.[20]

Other Indians carried out a more traditional existence, living with kin in indigenous villages. The seventy-five-year presence of the Spanish invaders had sufficiently damaged the environment and diminished local game that these native societies had to adapt. For example, the acquisition of horses enabled Indians to travel long distances quickly. Deteriorating food supplies forced previously peaceful Indians to become expert raiders. Such peoples became increasingly nomadic and warlike. Native groups frequently descended on Mexican settlements to raid for horses, cattle, and mules. However, they usually preferred to seize horses because of their value as a means of transportation, trade commodity, and food item. Ranchos near Los Angeles, Monterey, San Diego, and Santa Barbara were particularly susceptible to attack. One Plains MeWuk named Yozcolo conducted successful raids against the Mexican Californios for almost ten years. Native Americans outside of California also pillaged ranchos. Walkara, identified as a Ute but one who may have been Paiute or Chemehuevi, seized livestock annually from ranchos near San Bernardino, driving them north to Utah. Other Indian raiders carried on a brisk trade with Indians and non-Indians from New Mexico.[21]

Indian raids resulted in increased violence between Californios and native societies. Californios gained prominence by conducting military campaigns against indigenous peoples in the interior. Mariano Guadalupe Vallejo emerged both wealthy and powerful after he and his followers attacked and murdered over two hundred Wappos in 1834. By 1846, Mexico's Assembly passed resolutions calling for funds to pay Mexican citizens to locate and destroy Indian villages. Californio rancheros also employed Native Americans to crack down on livestock theft. For instance, the Lugo family of Rancho San Bernardino recruited Cahuilla Chief Juan Antonio and his people in the mid-1840s to guard the rancho's cattle and horses against Indian, Mexican, and white thieves. The alliance between the Lugo family and the Cahuillas was so strong that both groups joined forces on one occasion to kill approximately forty Luiseños and Cupeños.[22]

Rampant disease continued to be an acute problem for indigenous inhabitants of California during the Mexican period. Like other peoples throughout North America, the Indians of California had little or no immunity to European pathogens. Prior to 1827, diphtheria, measles, and pneumonia ravaged Indians living at the missions. In 1833, other maladies—such as cholera, smallpox, and syphilis—spread like wildfire. Approximately forty-five hundred Maidus, MeWuks, Wintuns, and Yokuts perished from various illnesses in that year alone. Some Mexican and white American immigrants to the region deliberately infected native peoples with these ailments, but other diseases spread unabated through the air and water as a result of non-Native contact. Native Americans struggled to comprehend the ferocity and mercilessness of these invisible killers. Between 1830 and 1848, almost 11,500 Native Americans died of "white man's diseases." By 1848, the population of Native California Indians was roughly 120,000, but it would decline radically during the era of the Gold Rush.[23]

CALIFORNIA INDIANS AND THE UNITED STATES

In the fifteen years prior to the war between the United States and Mexico, non-Spanish immigration to California accelerated. While most of the newcomers were Americans, John Sutter was a native of Switzerland who established a rancho at the confluence of the American and Sacramento rivers. Sutter built Rancho New Helvetia near several native villages, and the Swiss immigrant "contracted" local Indian peoples, treating them like serfs and offering them gifts for their labor. Native response to the Swiss immigrant varied. While some Indians expressed their disapproval of Sutter's presence by seizing his stock, others willingly worked for him. He and two MeWuk leaders, José Jesús and Polo, solidified an alliance in which Sutter provided the MeWuks with goods in exchange for their assistance against Indian raiders. José Jesús and Polo also regularly brought laborers to Sutter. This relationship appears to have benefited some people but caused resentment among some Indians living in the Sacramento Valley.[24]

While Sutter strengthened his ties with MeWuks, Mexican officials became concerned over the rising power of foreign rancheros who had no allegiance to Mexico. In the spring of 1846, General José Castro convinced the Muqueleme Indians to attack Sutter's rancho. Castro also hired a Muqueleme named Eusebio to murder Sutter. However, for one hundred dollars in assorted goods, MeWuks killed Eusebio before he could assassinate the Swiss ranchero. Such conflicts reflect the increasing tension between Californios and non-Spanish immigrants. This also demonstrates the complex relations between native societies and non-Indians.[25]

In May 1846, the United States declared war on Mexico. American civilians captured Sonoma one month later. Americans and Californios fought each other for control of southern California that fall. Native Americans reacted to these new circumstances in various ways, recalling their long history of oppression by the Spanish in California, some decided to side with the Americans. For instance, forty Tulare Indians joined John C. Frémont's battalion. Known as Company H, these Native Americans conducted numerous raids against Mexican ranchos. They successfully seized hundreds of Mexican cattle and horses. Others fought courageously beside Americans near Los Angeles in January 1847, forcing the Californios to surrender. Still others chose to take advantage of unprotected ranchos by stealing livestock for their own gain.[26]

With California claimed by Americans, military governor Stephen Watts Kearny dispatched soldiers to end Indian raids on livestock belonging to Californios. Carlos, a Yokuts chief, agreed to take Captain Henry Naglee and his troops to the accused raiders. Instead, he purposely led them in circles. On another occasion, Naglee's forces indiscriminately murdered two chiefs. The Americans hoped that Native Americans would discontinue their campaigns against ranchos, but Indians continued to steal livestock. Within months, animosity grew between Americans and some of the local native peoples.[27]

The year 1848 altered the lives of California's First Nations forever. The United States invaded California, wresting it from Native Americans and Mexicans who claimed it. Without the permission of Native Americans who held original title to their conquered lands, the United States formally "acquired" California under the Treaty of Guadalupe Hidalgo. Native Americans in California have contested the treaty since its ratification, arguing that they never surrendered their lands or their sovereignty. Indians argue that Spain and Mexico never "owned" California and the region did not belong to Mexico and thus could not be transferred to the United States. Americans seeking land and economic opportunity, have always ignored the native reality about the land and native sovereignty. Immigrants from the United States assumed ownership of California and began to trickle into the region after 1848.[28]

White immigrants brought with them hostile attitudes toward Indians which white Americans had developed from over 200 years of interaction with native peoples in the Eastern part of the country. Previously in California, the Spanish converted native peoples to Catholicism and tried to incorporate some Native Americans into Spanish and Mexican society. In addition, the Spanish and Mexicans had exploited native laborers, a well-worn tradition throughout Latin America. The incoming Americans surpassed Spaniards and Mexicans in their brutal treatment of Native Americans. For years, white Americans and their colonial forbears conquered and exterminated indigenous peoples of North America. Native Americans in the East did not remain idle but fought back and resisted white domination. However, most of the Eastern Woodland tribes lost their lands and peoples, resulting in a displacement of many peoples and forced removal of some Indians into the Indian Territory—present-day Kansas and Oklahoma. Most American immigrants to California viewed California's Indians in a manner comparable to the way they had viewed Indians in the East, obstacles that had to be relocated or annihilated. Yet through all this, Native Americans of California openly defied the American invaders and fought to defend their lands, cultures, and families.

CALIFORNIA'S GOLD RUSH

Another major event in 1848 caused thousands of Americans and people from all over the world to move to California. John Sutter decided to erect a sawmill in the late 1840s. He placed James Marshall in charge of selecting a site for the mill and to oversee its construction. In May 1847, an Indian guide led Marshall up the American River to a heavily-timbered area and a Maidu village called Coloma. As Marshall and the Maidus were on congenial terms, these Native Americans assisted in building the sawmill. While Maidus were digging a mill race along the American River on January 24, 1848, one of them uncovered gold. Maidus were already aware of the existence of gold, but they did not value it as a precious substance. Maidus, Nissenans, and other Native Americans of the Sierra Foothills working at Coloma had no idea of the significance of their discovery. They had no conception of its meaning in terms of their homes, families, and future. For Indians in California, the gold discovery at Coloma was a infamous event, one that would become a watershed in their history and that of many peoples of the world.[29]

The impact of the Gold Rush on Indians was tremendous. Some Native Americans living in or near the California foothills secured employment as miners. Rancheros hastened to the mining region, bringing with them Indian vaqueros and other native workers. Native laborers, as a result, quickly transformed from cowboys on the ranchos to gold miners in the Sierra Foothills. This was true in the case of Charles M. Weber, a rancher living near Stockton, who took his native employees into the foothills to pan for gold. During the early months of 1848, Weber and his Indian laborers journeyed to the mining camps, arriving at a mountainous area known as Dry Diggings (modern-day Placerville). Weber employed approximately one thousand Native Americans in hope of unearthing a bonanza of mineral wealth, and it was American Indian miners who found the first gold at Placerville. William Daylor from the Sacramento Valley soon joined Weber, and within a short time, the two men reportedly earned fifty thousand dollars off their Indian miners.[30]

Weber's optimism led him to hire Yokuts in the summer of 1848 to search for gold. Some of them worked at Dry Diggings, while others traveled south to what are now Calaveras and Stanislaus counties. Soon after, Yokuts discovered gold along Carson's Creek and Wood's Creek. This area eventually became known as the Southern Mines. The *Monterey Californian* reported that there were about three thousand Indians labored in the gold fields by August. Besides working on behalf of employers, some Native Americans staked out their own claims and labored for their own benefit, not for

Californios. An estimated four thousand Native Americans worked as miners by the end of 1848, including men, women, and children.[31]

Like most prospectors, Indians who participated in the first few years of the Gold Rush panned for placer gold. This method was probably the cheapest way to obtain gold, but it was back-breaking work. People also employed other methods to obtain the coveted mineral. Native American miners and others used a common instrument known as a "rocker." This contraption—somewhat resembled an infant's cradle and typically required three people to operate it. Workers placed it on an incline. One miner shoveled dirt into the hopper at the upper end, and another poured water on the dirt. The third person then rocked the apparatus, thereby forcing the mud through the rocker and out its lower end. Gold particles settled in the device's cleats. Yet the rocker was not totally effective or efficient, as small gold flakes often slid out with the tailings. By the fall of 1849, Indian miners used another contraption known as a "long tom." Functioning much like a rocker, this instrument enabled gold seekers to quickly wash large quantities of earth. It was usually about twelve feet in length. Prospectors channeled a stream of water through the long tom, thereby employing water to separate and sort through dirt and gravel. Long toms, some hundreds of feet long, were called sluices.[32]

White employers and merchants often cheated Native American laborers. For instance, Charles Weber and William Daylor paid native workers in goods, including blankets, coffee, clothing, meat, and sugar. These men and white traders greatly inflated the value of the goods, particularly in light of the value of the gold they unearthed. As a result, indigenous miners received meager compensation. Traders also cheated Indians, setting up stores near the gold fields and successfully swindling Indians and non-Indians alike. Self-employed Indians usually traded their gold at trading posts for rope, handkerchiefs, and cloth. As Native Americans could typically speak no English and only a little Spanish, merchants charged Indian miners exorbitant prices for goods. Several traders offered two prices for an item, the lower price for white miners and a higher price for Native Americans. Merchants commonly referred to the steeper rates as "Indian prices." When Indians insisted that they receive goods based on the weight of their gold, retailers used a two ounce weight, known as a "Digger Ounce," in order to secure gold from Native Americans at half its value. However, Indians soon realized the white man's love of gold and increasingly sought more equitable exchanges for this coveted mineral.[33]

KILLING INDIANS

Indian miners underwent dramatic changes during and after 1849. That year, people from all over the globe flooded into California. Thousands of Americans, French, Germans, Italians, Chinese, Chileans, Englishmen, Australians, and Mexicans converged on the mines hoping to obtain wealth beyond their wildest dreams. Even other Indians, including Cherokees and Wyandots, hurried to California to stake a claim. The influx of people brought a sharp increase in disease to the region, devastating indigenous peoples of California. Expanded mining activity disrupted the lives of thousands of Indians who had chosen not to participate in the Gold Rush but continued to lead traditional lifestyles. For these native men, women, and children of California's interior, their traditional food supplies sharply decreased and their streams became polluted. Lawless foreign adventurers appropriated Indian lands in order to uncover new gold deposits. The recent arrivals also considered native miners a menace, human obstacles to their own prosperity. Soon many newcomers viewed all Indians negatively and sought to exterminate them. Open conflict between the two groups resulted.[34]

In March 1849, a party of prospectors from Oregon attacked a Maidu village on the American River. These White invaders sexually assaulted many Maidu women and shot some of the Maidu men who attempted to intervene. Soon thereafter, Maidu warriors descended on a party of Oregon miners on the middle fork of the American River and killed five of them. About twenty white men from Oregon retaliated by forming a mob. This group of ruffians stormed an Indian village on Weber's Creek, killing at least twelve Native Americans and taking several prisoners. The Oregonians later brutally murdered eight of the Indian hostages. One visitor to California named William McCollum contended that whites from Oregon generally "hunt [Indians] as they would wild beasts."[35] James Marshall, who ascertained that many of the prisoners were his employees, was furious. The men from Oregon threatened Marshall's life and he retreated. George Parsons, a contemporary biographer of Marshall, asserted that the Native Americans butchered by the Oregon mob "belonged to a different tribe" of Indians than those who killed the five miners from Oregon. This mattered little to the whites from Oregon who blamed all Indians for the killings and indiscriminately retaliated against native people.[36]

Bayard Taylor, who visited the mining camps during the Gold Rush, wrote of another confrontation between whites and Native Americans in his book, *Eldorado*. California Indians unearthed gold near what is now Grinding Rock State Historical Park. After whites arrived, native Congenial relations prevailed

for several days until a white prospector accused Indians of stealing his pick.
A local chief agreed to visit the Indian mining camp to inquire about the missing tool. According to Taylor, as the indigenous leader hurried to the native
encampment, "one of the whites raised his rifle and shot him."[37] The white
miners gathered together, spread a false report that Native Americans had
murdered an innocent white man, and decided to drive the Indians out of the
rich region. California Indians retaliated by wounding a white man named
Aldrich with three arrows and then retreated into the nearby mountains.

These events had considerable impact on Native Americans in the mining
camps. California Indians recognized that the newcomers—jealous of their
lands, resources, and claims—wanted to annihilate them. The hostilities committed by whites forced Native American miners to withdraw en mass from
the gold fields. Indigenous societies not involved in mining also had to protect
themselves from future incursion, as many whites began murdering, burning,
and raping Indians. They also started kidnapping women and children, selling
them into slavery. White miners, no longer viewing the indigenous inhabitants
of California as productive employees, considered them a collective threat to
their prosperity or a commodity to be sold to the highest bidders.

Between 1849 and 1850, violence against California Indians escalated. An
incident known as the Clear Lake Massacre is a case in point. Two white men,
Andrew Kelsey and Charles Stone, established a ranch in the vicinity of Clear
Lake. They coerced several Pomo Indians to work for them. Kelsey and Stone
exploited, abused, and murdered some of their native laborers. In 1849, the
Pomos rose up and killed their oppressors. Whites blamed the entire affair on
the Indians, but the Pomos knew better and remember the incident well in
their own oral histories. American military forces, after hearing about Pomo
defiance, proceeded to the area to retaliate. The soldiers soon surrounded
about three hundred Native Americans on an island and began their assault.
Troops fired at any Indian in sight, killing dozens of non-combatants, including women, children, and elders. Captain Nathaniel Lyon—who led the massacre—described the island to which the Indians fled as "a perfect slaughter
pen."[38] Some American military officers and men in California, as in other
parts of the United States, felt that the only good Indian was a dead Indian,
and they put their beliefs into actions against the Pomos.

"PROTECTING" NATIVE CALIFORNIANS

Americans in the area as well as throughout the United States demanded
statehood for California. Under the Compromise of 1850, California entered
the union. The new California state legislature, dominated by whites from the

United States, passed statutes limiting the rights of "foreigners," which of course did not include white Americans. Whites in the Golden State wanted only white Americans to work in the gold fields. Under state law, miners who did not possess American citizenship had to pay a monthly fee of twenty dollars. This caused thousands of Mexicans to leave the mines. Many Chinese miners, however, initially paid the tax and continued to work, while other Chinese miners returned to San Francisco to begin anew. Angry at the recalcitrance of many Chinese miners to pay the tax and continue mining, xenophobic Americans taunted, beat, and murdered several Chinese miners. White miners and government officials clamored to rid the region of so-called foreigners as well as native people who competed with whites for limited gold.[39]

This general antipathy toward all non-whites, coupled by intensified white-Indian relations, resulted in the legal discrimination of California Indians. On April 22, 1850, the state legislature passed California Statute Chapter 133, known as "An Act for the Government and Protection of Indians." This series of twenty laws, similar to the Black Codes of the post-Civil War South, reflected the anti-Indian attitudes of whites during the mid-nineteenth century. For years, Americans had legislated against Native Americans at the state level. Generally speaking, Chapter 133 "legally" curtailed the rights of Native Americans in the Golden State and placed California Indians in a subordinate legal, political, social, and economic position within California's new society. The state laws significantly affected the lives of thousands of Indians for years, and the racist attitudes that initiated and executed these laws remain a part of the state's treatment of Native California Indians in contemporary society.[40]

Some of the statutes within this act influenced the course of Native Americans' history. Section 1, for instance, granted justices of the peace authority in all legal cases involving Native Americans. This ensured a dangerous amount of power at the municipal and county levels of government. White magistrates often despised Indians and deliberately favored local white citizens in cases involving land, resources, personal property, criminal offenses, and custody of children. Section 2 allowed the state to determine the residence of California's Native Americans, stating that Indians could continue to reside on indigenous lands. However, the provision stipulated that a justice of the peace could determine how much land Indians needed to survive and offer excess land—not deemed necessary for Native Americans—to be obtained by whites. Clearly, local judges possessed sufficient power to dispossess Native Americans of most of their homelands, including prime land in San Diego, Los Angeles, Santa Cruz, San Francisco, and other towns that emerged as major cities. Section 6 prohibited the native peoples of California from testifying against whites in a court of law. Indians, therefore, could not assist in convicting a white person through their own testimony. In civil cases, Native Americans could not testify against whites for burglary, land theft, cattle rustling, assault, battery, or other crimes. Whites simply stole land, livestock, and property from Native California Indians who had no legal recourse against white thieves. Worse yet, whites kidnapped Indian women and children, raping and committing other indignities for which Indians had no recourse under a legal system that denied them access.[41]

Other elements of this legislation sought to force Indians to work for whites. For example, Section 5 permitted white employers and Native American employees to enter into labor contracts. Indians, however, frequently did not understand the details of these agreements and remained in a state of perpetual servitude. According to Section 20, Native Americans who appeared to be "loitering and strolling about" would be arrested and incarcerated.[42] The definition of vagrancy under this law was highly subjective, depending on the interpretations of white justices of the peace who often incarcerated Indians. Virtually any white person could call on sheriffs, deputies, or marshals within cities or counties to arrest Indians who were unemployed or who had upset or inconvenienced a white person. Once the Indian was arrested and convicted, he or she was assessed a fine. When Indians could not pay their fines, officials allowed whites to pay the fine in return for the Indian's labor for a proscribed period of time. Section 14 allowed this transaction, permitting non-natives to post bond on Indian prisoners and legally force them to work for them, usually for four months. Under this legislation, abuse abounded. Whites were able to enjoy cheap and constant labor as well as dominate and frighten California's first people. American citizens and the California legislature worked together to compel Native Americans into oppressive labor relationships with whites.[43]

Chapter 133 was also a direct attack on native societies, and it was intended to establish and maintain white domination of native peoples. According to Section 10, Indians could not "set the prairie on fire, or refuse to use proper exertions to extinguish the fire when the prairies are burning." For years, indigenous inhabitants of California had set fire to their grasslands in order to draw game into canyons and other areas where Native American hunters could kill them. Burning the grass encouraged plant growth as well and was a form of range management. Without the ability to start range fires, the food supply for native peoples declined rapidly causing starvation. The invasion of thousands of non-Indians into California diminished local game and plant life, compelling some Native Americans to confiscate horses and livestock belonging to the newcomers for food. American Indians in California had been raiders for generations, but the destruction of the natural environment encouraged other Indians to steal and develop an economy based on livestock raiding. Indians were forced to steal or they would starve which was exactly what California's politicians and many citizens had in mind.[44]

Indian raids were a direct violation of Section 16 which prohibited Indians from stealing animals from whites. The state laws attempted to constrain the native peoples of California to completely abandon traditional practices while at the same time punishing them from stealing so that they could survive. This presented Indians with few options and justified white suppression and destruction of California's native population. Indians had no legal alternatives and were often dominated by whites or killed outright like animals. Section 13 of the law required indigenous leaders to turn over suspected Indian criminals to white officials. This section clashed with traditional Indian law which permitted local native leader to adjudicate wrongdoings. Moreover, Indian leaders well understood that there was no "justice" for native people through the courts. The law was also an assault on tribal and village authority and sovereignty that had rested with native peoples since the beginning of time. But Chapter 133 was intended by whites to destroy tribalism and place Native Americans into a subservient, dependent condition within California's racist society.[45]

TREATIES WITH CALIFORNIA'S INDIANS

Besides California state officials, the United States government also altered the lives of California Indians. During the 1840s and 1850s, the United States Army had men stationed in California, but the Army generally did nothing to protect the rights and lives of Native Americans in California. Instead, the Army allowed state officials, city fathers, county officers, and militia groups to murder, rape, and kidnap Indians. In addition, the national government, which had claimed primacy in Indian affairs since the Federalist period, did not exert itself in California. The newly formed Department of Interior and Office of Indian Affairs did not present a strong agenda in California, in spite of the fact that three officials negotiated eighteen treaties. In 1850, the federal government dispatched three commissioners—George Barbour, Redick McKee, and O. M. Wozencraft—to the Golden State to negotiate treaties with indigenous peoples. Considerable confusion surrounded the activities and instructions of these three officials, but they were the first federal officials to deal directly with the tribes in terms of treaties and reservations.[46]

Between 1851 and 1852, the three men concluded eighteen treaties with over one hundred native societies throughout the state. The negotiations were between sovereign governments or sovereign peoples—government to government relations. Indians did not passively submit to the demands of the United States. Instead, they negotiated doggedly with the Indian agents, thereby securing a portion of their aboriginal lands and some decent lands for their peoples. However, they lost vast acres of beautiful, productive, and bountiful land along the coast, in the valleys, throughout the mountains, and into the deserts—all land they once had controlled before the Spanish, Mexican, and American invasions. The agreements of the 1850s were significant in that they stipulated that Native Americans remove to reservations within California rather than relocate out of state. Under the accords, California's indigenous inhabitants were to retain approximately one-seventh of the state, but in the process, they lost millions of acres of their native estates.[47]

Most whites opposed the treaties because they asserted that the commissioners set aside lands too valuable for Indian occupation. Redick McKee attempted to pacify such objections by maintaining that "once the Indians adopted the food, clothing, and working habits of whites. . . . they would provide [whites] with vital labor for their mines and farms."[48] The governor of California, John Bigler, feared that establishing Indian reservations near American communities would result in violence. Other local officials regarded federal negotiations a violation of states' rights. Public pressure encouraged California's United States Senators to oppose ratification of all the treaties. In June 1852, the Senate formally rejected the eighteen treaties. Whites in California wanted all of the land and resources in the new state, and without federal recognition through the treaties, Indians had no legal relationship with the United States or federal protection of their lands. Without treaties, Indians in California were under the thumb of state laws that discriminated against them. Still, during the 1850s, some of the reservations created by the federal agreements functioned briefly. Other reservations emerged through acts of the Office of Indian Affairs operating within the state.

Prior to the arrival of Barbour, McKee, and Wozencraft in 1851, native societies in the Southern Mines challenged the invasion of miners into their territories. In December 1850, Yokuts raided James Savage's trading post on the Fresno River, stealing furniture, horses, mules, tents, and other items reportedly worth $25,000.[49] One week later, over one hundred Native Americans attacked a ferry crossing, killing one white person and stealing several horses and cattle. Yokut Indian leaders, José Rey and José Juarez, united native peoples in the region and conducted numerous campaigns against miners working the Southern Mines. Native California Indians killed at least twenty miners and wounded many others in an attempt to drive whites off their land. Between December 1850 and April 1851, Indians reportedly seized as much as $500,000 worth of livestock and goods, although this amount may have been inflated to encourage immediate and harsh reprisals against California's native population.[50]

State officials responded to the successful Indian raids by authorizing the creation of a volunteer military force known as the Mariposa Battalion. This unit of militia soldiers soon arrived in the Southern Mines and harassed native peoples, whether or not they had been involved in the recent raids. As a result of these attacks, several Indian leaders negotiated with the three federal Indian commissioners because native leaders believed it in their best interest to do so. Yosemite MeWuk and Chowchilla Indians refused to speak with the agents, while at the same time, they evaded the Mariposa Battalion. Tenaya, one prominent Yosemite leader, never signed a treaty with the Americans. Many Indians who entered into such agreements frequently bolted the temporary reservations, preferring to live in their mountain homelands. As a result, the California state legislature appropriated over $1.5 million during the 1850s for local troops to fight indigenous peoples who were unwilling to remove to the reservations and live under federal domination.[51]

CALIFORNIA INDIAN RESISTANCE

While whites typically sought to exploit, harass, or exterminate indigenous peoples of the Golden State, the newspapers on a few occasions offered an honest assessment of the plight of California's Indians. The *Alta California* printed one such article—one which likely fell on deaf ears. The anonymous journalist began the essay by defining the relationship of California's native peoples to their lands. The Indians "are the original possessors of the soil," an editor pointed out, for the earth holds "all the associations of their lives" and "their traditions." Afterward, the author blamed avaricious miners for driving out local game, desecrating indigenous grave sites in search of "the glittering gold which lay beneath," and mercilessly robbing and murdering native peoples. The writer also related how whites "pushed [Indians] from the valleys where their arrows procured their meat, from the rivers where they caught their fish, . . . [and from] their oak orchards."[52] Despite this eloquent plea for whites to end hostilities against Native Americans, white Americans—as previously mentioned—organized the Mariposa Battalion to destroy native men, women, and children.

Native Americans answered white depredations by raiding Americans whenever possible. In February 1853, Indian peoples attacked a pack train bound for Yreka. They killed a white man named Dick Owen, but another man, one Mr. Archer, managed to escape. The Indians seized a horse and thirteen mules, including the supplies each animal carried. Before withdrawing, these Indians also attacked another train, wounding a number of mules.[53] Such campaigns, though completely justified, enraged whites. According to the *Alta California*, "Indians have committed so many depredations in the North, of late, that . . . [whites] are ready to knife them, shoot them, or inoculate them with small pox—all of which have been done."[54]

In addition to indigenous peoples near the gold fields, other Indians in the Golden State opposed the ever-increasing presence of American citizens. Native Americans retaliated against the numerous white invaders who seemed to engage in hostilities and stir up trouble wherever they went. John Glanton, a Texan of questionable character, stole a ferry business from Able Lincoln on the Colorado River. He and his associates charged exorbitant fees for passage across that desert waterway and wanted to eliminate all competition. In April 1850, some Americans passing through the region disapproved of Glanton's inflated prices and decided to construct their own ferry. These American travelers crossed the Colorado on their vessel and then offered the boat to local Quechan Indians. The Native Americans began their own ferry operation in direct competition with Glanton.[55]

According to the *Alta California*, Glanton and his men "marched down to the Indian[s'] ferry, seized their boat and destroyed it." They also grabbed "an Irishman [one Callahan], whom the Indians had enlisted in their service, tied his hands and heels together, and threw him into the Colorado." The Quechans assembled and "determined that the Americans must die."[56] Waiting for an opportune moment, the Indians struck Glanton's camp while he and his men slept off a drunk. Historian Donald Jackson states that Glanton and ten Americans died in the attack, and Harvey Johnson, the most celebrated historian of the lower Colorado River confirmed that while the Quechans killed the Texans, two ferrymen watched in horror and walked from the river to San Diego to announce the "massacre."[57] A militia group led by Major Joseph G. Morehead organized to punish the Quechans, but the Quechans counterattacked these irregular forces, surrounding them in a small stockade previously built by new ferry operators. If it had not been for the stockade and the new ferrymen working at the Yuma Crossing, Quechans likely would have annihilated Moorehead and his makeshift troops.[58]

White migration to California not only affected Indian-white relations, but also influenced the formation of alliances between indigenous groups. For example, a pan-Indian resistance movement developed in southern California in 1851. Antonio Garra, a primary leader of the Cupeños, intended to drive the Americans from the area. He solicited the support of various Cahillas, Kumeyaays, Luiseños, and Quechans. His plans centered on attacking Camp Independence (just west of Fort Yuma on the Colorado River at the base of Pilot Knob), Los Angeles, San Diego, and Santa Barbara. Garra's warriors burned the Rancho of Juan José Warner, an American who exploited Cupeño workers, but the war did not develop beyond Warner's ranch. Although many Indians were outraged by the growing American presence, few joined the armed resistance. The prominent Cahuilla leader Juan Antonio opposed Garra, most likely because the two men—both powerful within the native communities of the desert—were at odds with each other.[59] Juan Antonio ultimately captured Garra, presenting him to local authorities. A military tribunal convicted and executed Garra. His multi-tribal alliance broke down, and Native Americans sought other ways to resist.[60]

IMAGES OF CALIFORNIA'S INDIANS

Most foreign immigrants arriving in California blamed Native Americans for most murders and other crimes. Americans and their newspapers portrayed the image that Indians were responsible for most acts of violence in the state. For instance, the *Alta California* reported that one "murder of an atrocious character was perpetrated by some persons, probably Indians," in San Diego on the night of January 13, 1853. The newspaper graphically described how the body of George Warren "was found stripped nearly naked, . . . and his brains literally beaten out." People at the crime scene discovered a "jaw bone of an ox . . . near [the white person's corpse] covered with blood, brains and mangled masses of flesh and hair." After providing this gory depiction, the author of this article cast swift judgments. "Suspicion points to certain Indians last seen in his company, who undoubtedly murdered the poor wretch for the sake of the miserable clothing he wore." The report concluded that San Diego "is infested with a gang of Indian thieves and murderers, who should be driven out."[61] Thus, a mysterious murder instantly became a rallying cry to expel all American Indians from this part of southern California.

Americans also attributed murders in and near the gold fields to Indians. One Mr. Slater, a rancher, disappeared for a number of days. According to the *Alta California,* an anonymous person found Slater's body "much eaten by wolves." The paper recalled that the white man's "head, arms and legs had been carried away, and not enough left to identify him, had he not been previously missed." Again, the *Alta California* "supposed that the deed was done by the Indians." The American press in California recounted such scenes in gruesome detail in hope of casting Native Americans as savage brutes who killed whites for no reason. This image of native California Indians justified the theft of Indian land and resources. It also encouraged the destruction of Indian people and their cultures, depicting native peoples as barbaric savages who deserved to be extinguished from the earth in order to make way for superior, civilized people. Such appalling reports as that presented above horrified whites and significantly influenced their attitudes toward California Indians.[62]

California's Reservation System

While whites continued to view the Native Americans of California as scapegoats, the federal government attempted to deal with the state's so-called "Indian problem." However, federal control of Indians affairs in California was poorly orchestrated in the 1850s and 1860s as state and local officials assumed superiority in Indian affairs. In March 1852—three months before the United States Senate turned down the treaties of Barbour, McKee, and Wozencraft—Congress created the office of superintendent of Indian affairs of California. The president appointed Edward F. Beale to that position, and in September 1852, Beale arrived in the Golden State to assume his duties. He eventually established an Indian reservation system that in many respects resembled the efforts of Barbour, McKee, and Wozencraft. He hired Indian agents to reside near reservation Indians and ideally wanted a military post to be located adjacent the reservation. However, in contrast to the three commissioners, Beale organized smaller reservations in areas not heavily populated by whites which were each approximately seventy-five thousand acres in size. After Congress appropriated a total of $350,000 during 1852 and 1853, the superintendent commenced his operation.[63]

In 1853, Beale created California's first official reservation near Tejon Pass at the southern end of the San Joaquin Valley. Beale created the first reservation system in the United States, the prototype for future "modern" reservations designed to "civilize" Indians through agriculture and ranching regulated by agents of the Office of Indian Affairs. The next year he proudly reported that Tulare first reservation system in the United States, the prototype for future "modern" reservations designed to "civilir or complaint, but with the most cheerful alacrity." He further stated that "as the fruits of their labor begin to show itself [sic] in the immense field . . ., [the Indians] look at it in amazement, and with delight."[64] If Beale is reporting accurately, these California Indians were enjoying the reservation life as farmers, but Beale took the credit for the initial success at Tejon, failing to mention that the Tulareños did all the work involved in raising crops. Soon soldiers forced nonagricultural Indians to relocate to the Tejon Reservation.[65]

The drastic change in lifestyle for California's native peoples from freedom to confinement onto reservations where they faced strict discipline and foreign domination caused several Native Americans to flee the reservation for sanctuary in their traditional homelands. The reservation at Fort Tejon eventually failed, closing in 1864, but the concept of Beale's reservation system lived on into the twentieth century. Out of the 1850s and after the Civil War, the United States embarked on a national reservation policy of forcing Indians onto confined areas where agents of the Office of Indian Affairs could controll them. The government isolated Indians onto reservations, diminishing their freedoms, and concentrating diverse peoples onto small land bases where agents could "civilize" them through farming and Christianization. Once corralled and confined, the government permitted non-Indians to resettle former Indian lands, legally securing title to it and prohibiting Indians from living on or using their traditional homelands or resources. This became the national model for reservations from the mid-nineteenth century to the twentieth century, and this national policy, with traditions in the American past, emerged full-bloom in California.[66]

One year after the creation of the reserve at Fort Tejon, Beale's successor— Thomas J. Henley—established the Nome Lackee and Fresno reservations. Henley later founded the Klamath and Medicino reservations in 1855. In addition, he created two "Indian farms." On these farms and reservations, agents taught Native Americans how to cultivate vast tracts of land. Almost ten thousand of the state's fifty thousand Indians lived under this paternalistic system in 1857. Echoing the events at Fort Tejon, Indians loathed the conditions at the other reservations and escaped in droves during the late 1850s and early 1860s. California newspapers, initially printed rave reviews of the reservations and the grand harvests there, but the newspapers soon began writing alarming critiques as the "truth" of the failures became apparent. One by one, the Office of Indian Affairs closed reservations. By the end of the 1860s, all of the five original reservations created in the mid-1850s were no longer in operation. Only three others—the Tule River, Round Valley, and Hoopa Valley reservations—remained.[67]

Dismal conditions prevailed on the reservations in California. Through the patronage system, corrupt and incompetent men often became Indian agents. These men received cash appropriations from the federal government to purchase decent rations for reservation Indians. Instead of fulfilling this obligation, Indian agents frequently acquired blankets, cattle, food, and supplies of inferior quality and then pocketed the remaining funds. Meat was often rancid by the time Indians on the reserves obtained it. For these native peoples, they could either remain on the reservations and starve to death or leave and live as their ancestors or raid non-native communities and ranches for horses, cattle, and other livestock. They often chose the latter.[68]

CALIFORNIA INDIAN HOLOCAUST AND SURVIVAL

Whites, however, failed to recognize that Indians really had no choice but to flee the reservations. It was a question of survival. American citizens forgot that whites had polluted the streams and rivers, drove off or killed local game, and disrupted traditional societies. In essence, the actions of whites compelled many of California's Indians to steal cattle and horses. Whites viewed reservations as a place to concentrate, confine, and control Indians so that non-native peoples could develop the state in a manner they saw fit. When Indians left the reservations to raid local ranches, whites retaliated swiftly— even without legal authority. For instance, a volunteer militia group in Fresno and Tulare counties forcibly assembled approximately two hundred Yokuts during the fall of 1858. The militia destroyed native villages and forced the men, women, and children onto the Fresno Reservation. This vigilante group carried out this action, because these Indians had reportedly stolen pigs and cattle from local ranchers. At least this was their justification for forcing them off their traditional homelands and onto the government reservation. In this way, the militia force could open Indian lands for white to resettle, claiming choice lands near water resources while at the same time corralling their native enemies.[69]

Military campaigns against native societies typically involved the indiscriminate murders of several Indians and forcing survivors onto reservations. One Captain Jarboe, for example, proudly proclaimed that within four months he and his cohorts had killed 283 Indians and escorted 292 others to Mendocino Reservation.[70] There are no records regarding how many native women and children were raped, kidnapped, or sold into slavery. Some white Americans openly committed genocide, killing many Indians to drive them from the land and exterminate them. This was their intention, and racism mixed with economic gain combined to cause a deadly mixture for native men, women, and children. In order to encourage the extermination of California's First Nations, white individuals and communities offered monetary rewards for the heads and scalps of Indian people.

Indeed, Shasta City awarded five dollars for each Indian head presented to municipal officials. Residents of Honey Lake paid twenty-five cents per Indian scalp in 1863. Volunteer militia groups of cut throats murdered Indians indiscriminately and turned their body parts into cash money while at the same time, cleared the land of its original inhabitants. Concentration of Indians on reservations posed problems for native people other than starvation, for they were easy targets for white vigilantes and scalp hunters. As a result, the bloody and vicious cycle continued in California, as Indians jumped the reservations, stole livestock to survive, and fought disgruntled whites. Native California Indians either died in their fight for survival off the reservations or returned to the reservations to await attack or death by starvation.[71]

During the 1860s, California Indians did not willingly submit to white power or vigilantism but fought for their families and people against the foreign invaders and murderers. In 1862, Native Americans in the Coso Mining District in Owens Valley forced whites to abandon the area for a year. In the same year, Indians in Humboldt County conducted successful raids on white communities that caused non-natives to desert many farms and ranches. Native peoples burned American homes and farms, and such campaigns effectively hampered the economic development of the region by whites. Indians also captured whites during raids. In the summer of 1862, Yahis kidnapped three white children. Likely retaliating for the murder of Yahi infants, these Indians killed two of the young hostages. Whites eventually discovered one of the slain children with seventeen arrows in him, his throat slit, and his head scalped. Innocent children—Indian and non-Indian—were truly the victims in these wars initiated and conducted by adults. Clearly, both Native Americans and whites committed heinous acts against helpless youngsters, and both justified their actions within their own communities. However, whites generally had the upper hand, killing and kidnapping far more people and selling them into slavery.[72]

White militia groups during the 1860s continued to hunt down and destroy native peoples. In 1860, whites living in Humboldt County attacked a number of the local Indian villages. The Americans endeavored to annihilate indigenous peoples in retaliation for cattle and other items taken in raids. Native men often were not in the villages at the time of these attacks, owing to the fact that whites preferred to wait for them to leave the villages before commencing hostilities. According to the San Francisco *Bulletin*, "bands of white men, armed with hatchets . . .[,] fell on the women and children, and deliberately slaughtered them, one and all." One witness to these atrocities counted twenty-six bodies of women and children in one camp. The *Bulletin* discussed the victims of this mindless assault. "Some of them were infants at the breast," one editor wrote, "whose skulls had been cleft again and again." The writer of this newspaper account was highly critical of the whites who participated in this carnage, referring to these cowards as "the lowest and most brutal of the border population." The anonymous journalist asserted that the whites who precipitated the attack "possess nothing of humanity but the form and the bestial instincts."[73]

NADIR AND SURVIVAL

By 1870, the native population had declined to 20,000 from 40,000 people. The killing and kidnapping of California's first peoples had been great. Some Indians that died during the era of the Gold Rush California succumbed to bacteria and viruses brought by foreigners who invaded the region, as diseases spread throughout the gold fields and onto the reservations. Yet volunteer militia units murdered thousands of Native Americans, and enslaved thousands more. Non-native immigrants to California from many parts of the world brought their racist attitudes with them to California, mixing their racism with their greed to produce bloody violence against a people the outsiders generically labeled "Diggers." The foreigners denigrated California's Indians in their writings, depicting native people much as they would wild animals who aimlessly "roamed" the land like herds with no social organizations, governments, laws, or religions. This was the biased image that whites intended to portray of a people they wanted removed from the land or exterminated completely.

Despite the efforts of some whites to exterminate the native peoples of California, American Indians in California survived the holocaust. They have survived in spite of one hundred and fifty years of racial hatred and discrimination which forced them off their lands and marginalized them throughout the state. They have survived civilization programs, Christianity, forced removals to reservations, and rape of their lands and resources. In spite of obscene death rates during the twentieth century caused by tuberculosis, pneumonia, sudden infant death syndrome, and numerous other health problems, they have survived. And California's Indians continue to survive in spite of a state government that has discriminated against them since 1850 and continues to deny them educational opportunities and a measure of economic prosperity through the gaming industry.[74]

At the end of the twentieth century, there are roughly 200,000 Native Americans living in the Golden State, and many of them are watching with interest as the state launches its sesquicentennial of the California Gold Rush. While the governor, legislators, representatives, and senators make much political hay of the Gold Rush, California's Indian people are not celebrating. They are remembering the genocide of their people, the rape of their women and children, and the enslavement of their family members who helped build the Golden State. For California's First Nations, the era of the Gold Rush was truly a holocaust, a watershed in their history that they remember through their oral histories and numerous written accounts left by non-natives who watched and recorded the horror.

EDITING WRITTEN ACCOUNTS

The editors have made every effort to reproduce the accounts found herein as accurately as possible. However, several editorial problems have emerged that readers should be cognizant of before analyzing the documents below. Spelling, punctuation, use of nouns and verbs, and use of the English language is not always consistent with contemporary dictionaries or grammar. For example, some writers use semicolons-colons instead of commas, or they use hyphens instead of periods. Sometimes writers broke words that are not broken today such as any thing or hyphens in between such words as any-thing. Sometimes writers italicized the names of other newspapers and sometimes they do not. Rarely do editors italicize the names of ships in accordance with rules of grammar today. The documents emerged out of the mid-nineteenth century when newspaper reporters and editors as well as military and civilian writers had varying degrees of education. Often the articles are written in an awkward fashion or by writers who use colloquial phases that are difficult to understand today. In addition, many of the articles have been taken from microfilm that is extremely difficult to read due to missing words, smudges, and dark dots that obscure the text. None of this diminishes the significance of the accounts or their importance as historical sources.

The original and classic works of Robert F. Heizer and Alan Almquist—published by Ballena Press, Peregine Smith, and the University of California—have been out of print for over twenty years. One of the objectives of this work was to introduce them again to the general public and a new generation with the sincere hope that they may alter the way in which the history of California during the Gold Rush era is presented in schools and colleges. The work may also encourage scholars to rethink genocide among California's native peoples.

NOTES

1. *Chico Courant,* July 28, 1866.
2. James J. Rawls, "Gold Diggers: Indian Miners in the California Gold Rush," *California Historical Quarterly* 55 (Spring 1976): 29–30; James J. Rawls, *Indians of California: The*

Changing Image (Norman: University of Oklahoma Press, 1984): 116–17. Rawls has conducted the most recent and comprehensive research on the Gold Rush era. For a work intended for young readers, see Clifford E. Trafzer, *California Indians and the Gold Rush* (Newcastle, California: Sierra Oaks Publishing Company, 1989): 1–6.

3. See Mason's report in House Executive Document 1, 30th Congress, 2nd Session, 60.

4. William Kelly, *An Excursion to California over the Prairie, Rocky Mountains, and Great Sierra Nevada. . . .* 2 (London: Chapman and Hall, 1851): 45.

5. The best discussion of the developing conflict between California's Indians and Oregonians is Rawls, "Gold Diggers," 36–39.

6. For a general discussion of Eastern Indians, see Clifford E. Trafzer, *As Long as the Grass Shall Grow: Native American History, 1400–2000* (New York: Harcourt Brace, 1999). For the quote, see Richard L. Carrico, *Strangers in a Stolen Land: American Indians in San Diego, 1850–1880* (Newcastle, California: Sierra Oaks Publishing Company, 1987): 18–36.

7. For general information about the cultures of California's Indians, see Alfred L. Kroeber, *Elements of Culture in Native California* (Berkeley: University of California Press, 1922); Alfred L. Kroeber, *Handbook of the Indians of California* (Washington, D. C.: Smithsonian Institution Press, 1925); Robert F. Heizer, editor, *California: Handbook of North American Indians* 8 (Washington, D. C.: Smithsonian Institution Press, 1978); Rupert Costo and Jeannette Henry Costo, *Natives of the Golden State: The California Indians* (San Francisco: The Indian Historian Press, 1995).

8. Ibid.

9. Oral interview, Clifford E. Trafzer with Darryl Babe Wilson, 1992.

10. Hubert Howe Bancroft, *History of California*, 7 vols. (San Francisco: The History Company, 1886): 1–64.

11. Ibid., 110–25.

12. Ibid.; Edward D. Castillo, "The Impact of Euro-American Exploration and Settlement," in Heizer, ed., *California*, 99–104. Hereafter cited as Castillo, "The Impact."

13. For a general study of the missions, see Edith B. Webb, *Indian Life at the Old Missions* (Lincoln: University of Nebraska Press, 1952). Also see this volume intended for young audiences, Clifford E. Trafzer, *American Indians as Cowboys* (Newcastle, California: Sierra Oaks Publishing Company): 11–17.

14. Jayme to Serra, October 17, 1772 in Maynard Geiger, ed., Baja Travel Series (Los Angeles: Dawson's Book Shop, 1970): 43–44.

15. Rawls, *Indians of California*, 25–43.

16. Bancroft, *History of California*, 251–53; Castillo, "The Impact," 102–4.

17. Clifford E. Trafzer, *Yuma: Frontier Crossing of the Far Southwest* (Wichita, Kansas: Western Heritage Books, 1980): 15–21.

18. Castillo, "The Impact," 103.

19. Ibid., 105–6.

20. George Harwood Phillips, *Chiefs and Challengers* (Berkeley: University of California Press, 1975): 37–39.

21. Ibid., 43; Paul Bailey, *Walkara* (Los Angeles: Westernlore Press, 1954).

22. Castillo, "The Impact," 105–6; Phillips, *Chiefs and Challengers*, 45–62.

23. Castillo, "The Impact," 106.

24. Rawls, *Indians of California*, 77–79.

25. Bancroft, *History of California,* 6: 12–17.

26. Ibid., 5: 1–29.

27. Ibid.

28. Castillo, "The Impact," 107.

29. Bancroft suggests that a California Indian named Jim may have discovered the gold, while Rawls points out that Marshall first claimed that he had found it and later acknowledged that whites and Indians found the gold. Rawls, "Gold Diggers," 29–30; William McCollum, *California As I Saw It,* edited by Dale E. Morgan (Los Gatos, California: The Talisman Press, 1960): 147.

30. Bancroft, *History of California,* 6: 67–81.

31. Ibid., 82–109, 351–80.

32. Ibid., 409–28.

33. Rawls, "Indian Diggers," 34–36; Trafzer, *California Indians and the Gold Rush,* 28–34.

34. Trafzer, *California Indians and the Gold Rush,* 34–39.

35. McCollum, *California As I Saw It,* 147.

36. George Frederic Parsons, *The Life and Adventures of James W. Marshall* (Sacramento, California: James W. Marshall and W. Burke, 1870): 113.

37. Bayard Taylor, *Eldorado* (New York: Alfred A. Knopf, 1949): 185.

38. Nathaniel Lyon to E. R. S. Canby, May 22, 1850, National Archives, Records of the War Department, Document 329a, Record Group 98, Letters Received, 1850, as found in Robert F. Heizer, ed., *The Destruction of California Indians* (Santa Barbara: Peregrine Smith, Inc., 1974): 245.

39. Robert F. Heizer and Alan F. Almquist, *The Other Californians* (Berkeley: University of California Press, 1971): 121, 145–46, 151, 154, 156.

40. Ibid., 39–40; California Statute 133, "An Act for the Government and Protection of Indians, Statutes of California, April 22, 1850. Hereafter cited as California Statute 133. See S. Garfielde and F. A. Snyder, compilers, *Compiled Laws of California* (Benicia, California: S. Garfielde, 1853): 825. In this compilation, the law is known as Chapter 150. Also see, Carrico, *Strangers in a Stolen Land,* 38–40.

41. California Statute 133.

42. Ibid.

43. Ibid.

44. Ibid.

45. Ibid.

46. Heizer and Almquist, *The Other Californians,* 68–81.

47. Ibid.

48. George Harwood Phillips, *Indians and Indian Agents* (Norman: University of Oklahoma Press, 1997): 164–65.

49. Savage was an Anglo American who immigrated to California in 1846. With the discovery of gold, he used Indians to get rich. Then he made greater wealth by establishing three trading posts at the Southern Mines.

50. Phillips, *Indians and Indian Agents,* 37–56, 78–91; Rawls, *Indians of California,* 185; Costillo, "The Impact of Euro-American Exploration and Settlement," 108

51. Heizer and Almquist, *The Other Californians,* 67–85.

52. *Alta California,* January 15, 1851.

53. Ibid., March 2, 1853.

54. Ibid., March 6, 1853.
55. Trafzer, *Yuma*, 52, 74–77.
56. Ibid.; *Alta California*, January 8, 1851.
57. Donald Dale Jackson, *Gold Dust* (New York: Alfred A. Knopf, 1980): 268. Harvey Johnson was the foremost scholar on the history of the Colorado River and worked for years as a volunteer for the Yuma County Historical Society. His work on the Glanton gang and Quechan attack are represented in Trafzer, Yuma, 74–77.
58. Trafzer, *Yuma*, 52, 76. See also the Johnson Collection, Yuma County Historical Society, Yuma, Arizona.
59. Oral interview, Clifford E. Trafzer with Katherine Saubel, 1997.
60. Phillips, *Chiefs and Challengers*, 170.
61. *Alta California*, February 21, 1853.
62. Ibid., April 1, 1853.
63. Rawls, *Indians of California*, 148–50.
64. As quoted in Rawls, *Indians of California*, 151.
65. Ibid., 148–50.
66. Clifford E. Trafzer, *The Kit Carson Campaign: The Last Great Navajo War* (Norman: University of Oklahoma Press, 1982): 224–37.
67. Rawls, *Indians of California*, 152.
68. Ibid.
69. Ibid.
70. Ibid., 164.
71. Ibid., 185.
72. Ibid., 182.
73. *San Francisco Bulletin*, June 18, 1860, as quoted from Heizer, ed., *The Destruction of California Indians*, 254.
74. Clifford E. Trafzer, Luke Madrigal, and Anthony Madrigal, Chemehuevi People of the Coachella Valley (Coachella, California: Chemehuevi Press, 1997): 117–24.

★ ★

WHITE AMERICAN PERCEPTIONS OF CALIFORNIA INDIANS

This chapter includes a series of documents that offer superb insight into the attitudes of whites toward the Native Americans of California. As Anglos moved rapidly into the Gold Rush, they brought with them racial prejudices regarding North American Indians. Over two hundred years of interaction between whites and Native Americans shaped and influenced these views. By the time of the Gold Rush, most whites despised Indians. They considered the indigenous inhabitants of North America to be godless, barbaric, and savage. To a majority of whites, Native Americans had no redeeming value and stood as barriers to American "civilization" and progress. In California, whites referred to Indians as Diggers, a pejorative term closely related to "nigger." Anglos wanted Indians pushed out of the way or exterminated. Only enlightened whites favored reservations where Indians could be civilized.

Many of the following newspaper articles echo these negative sentiments about Indians. Some of the reports recount murders. A few journalists assume that Native Americans committed the heinous acts, yet the writers provide no concrete evidence to support their claims. They suppose that only Indians kill people in California. These accounts portray native peoples of the Golden State as bloodthirsty, ruthless barbarians.

Other documents incorporate divergent views regarding Native Americans. Some Americans during this period advocated a so-called Christian solution to the supposed "Indian problem." A few more sympathetic—yet still highly paternalistic—treatments depict Indians as being immoral, depraved heathens who must move to reservations so that they can learn Christianity and become "civilized." However, a few reports actually attempt to view Anglo hostilities from the Indians' perspectives. These outline the loss of indigenous homelands and hunting-gathering-fishing territories and acknowledge the necessity for Native Americans to steal food and supplies in order to survive. Still other reports propose that Indians are primitive people destined to become extinct. White perceptions and preconceived notions of native Californians made it easier for nonwhites to disregard Indian rights, steal Indian lands, and murder innocent people.

Daily Alta California, January 18, 1849
SACRAMENTO CITY, Jan. 4th, 1849

"Yesterday we were all agog with a report which came in, that some wagoners, (some eight), were fighting with some Indians at the fork of the road between here and the "dry diggins [*sic*]," three or four miles this side of the log cabin at the "Green Spa." Some say a wagon broke down, and that while one of the teamsters went to get help or another wagon, the other stopped to guard the broken one—that some Indians came about and a fight arose—that the other teamster and some other men came up, and a general fight took place—that the Indians ran, and that the whites burnt their rancherias, which it seems were near. Others say that the Indians had stolen an ox, and that the whites wished to punish them. The proof that they stole the ox, is, that his tracks were found leading *to* the rancheria, but were not found going *away* from it.

To-day when I came in from work, I found the people all astir, in consequence of an express having arrived from Leidsdorff's ranch, saying some Indians had been to a camp near, and driven off eight white men, (Oregonians.) Everybody who could raise a horse turned out to go to their relief—They were just returning. They said the excitement was caused by the following circumstances:

Yesterday an old Indian, well known in this neighborhood, and who had a good character came to a camp of Oregonians, and one of them claimed one of his horses. The Indian said he had bought the horse from a white man, and did not like to give him up-showed the fresh "*vent,*" &c. The white man persisted that he was his horse, and took him away from him. The Indian was enraged, and rode off, making use of expressions which were not agreeable to the Oregonian, and he took up his rifle and shot him. The Indian's horse went home, his saddle covered in blood, but without his rider. Today, some time, armed Indians came to the camp of, or met some eight Oregonians, and the latter knowing the occurrence of yesterday, *presumed* they had come to take revenge, and gave them battle, and were whipped. One of them came in to the Fort and told his story, and the whole garrison turned out to their rescue, but when they returned, having heard other stories, they were pretty generally sorry the Indians had not whipped them worse."

"Notice was given, that to-night there would be a meeting to take into consideration the propriety of organising [sic] a provisional government."

Daily Alta California, January 18, 1849
An Indian Fight

We learn verbally that a man named James M. Vail, a discharged volunteer of the 1st N. Y. Regt., and who was attached to Capt. Shannon's company of miners, is supposed to have been taken prisoner by the Indians, and fears are entertained that he has been murdered. It appears that a few mornings after the party reached Weaver's creek, Vail went out to fell trees for building a log house. As he did not return that night, a party went in pursuit of him the next day, but discovered no trace of him. The following day the search continued, the party discovering smoking ruins of a large rancheria, and finding tracks of shoes, among others, going farther into the mountains. This trail was followed without success, the party overtaking and killing an Indian. It is supposed that the Indians have murdered Vail, and fearing the consequences, have burned their wigwams and retired into the mountains. It is barely possible, however, from the shoe tracks, that they may have driven him with them into captivity.

Daily Alta California, January 15, 1851
Our Indian Difficulties

It is to be hoped that the temperate and reasonable address of the Indian Agents, which we published yesterday, may have weight with the public, and induce that forbearance and moderation which the importance of the matter demands. Not only do we hope that the miners and people generally will pause and let reason and justice guide their conduct toward the ignorant starving savages, but that our legislators and all those who hold public and high trust will use their influence to prevent the effusion of blood. It is not for the benefit of our State, viewed even in a pecuniary light, to annihilate these poor creatures. But there are reasons infinitely beyond all estimated dollars and cents, all prospects of profitable business or possessions, which should guide our councils and conduct. There is a question of justice, of humanity, of right, of religion. They are the original possessors of the soil. Here are all the associations of their lives. Here are their traditions. The trees which we cut down are the volumes of their unwritten histories. The mountain-tops are their temples; the running streams which we turn aside for gold have been the store-houses of their food, their fisheries by us destroyed and their supplies cut off.

The wild game, which gave them food we have driven from the valleys, the very graves of their sires have been dug down for the glittering gold which lay beneath. The reckless of our people have not stopped at these inevitable results. They have abused and outraged the confidence and friendship of the trusting Indians, robbed and murdered them without compunction, and, in short, perpetrated all those outrages against humanity, and decency, and justice, which have entailed upon the American public nearly every war which has turned red with Indian blood the green vallies [sic] from the Pequod and Narragansett nations, all the way through the continent, which we have taken from them, to the sand-bordered homes of the Yumas, and the oaten hills of the Clear Lake tribes.

Is it not time to pause and inquire if might is right in this matter? We make war upon them and annihilate them. But is that the best policy? Is it humane? Is it polite? It is Christian? We answer it is not. The Indian has his vices; it is to be regretted that the white man has many—ay, greater by far than these poor children of nature. And is it known, too, that they have lived on the most friendly terms with us until oppression has broken all the bonds between the races?

We have driven them to the wall. We have pushed them from the valleys where their arrows procured their meat, from the rivers where they caught their fish, we have destroyed their oak orchards; we have cut down or burned their wheat which was the seed of the wild grass; have slaughtered the men and debauched the women. And now the atonement is to be, utter destruction! Can God look down upon such cruelty, and bless the people guilty of the outrage? We therefore call once more for the moderation of council and moderation in action. Our agents are already upon the mission. Let all good citizens give a helping hand. Let us avoid if within the bounds of possibility, an Indian war. Such a calamity would not alone be one to the Indians. It will cost the lives of many valuable citizens. And should it end in the total destruction of the Indian tribes, it would be at a cost of treasure and blood horrible to contemplate, for which there could be no adequate return, and would be a result over which the Philanthropist, the Christian, and every true hearted man would mourn as the last great sin of national injustice, violence, and oppression.

Daily Alta California, January 20, 1851
Los Angeles Correspondence
LOS ANGELES, Dec. 1850

Messrs. Editors: On Sunday last an Indian was brought into town and committed to jail, charged with committing a rape upon one of his female companions and afterward killing her. The same night a Sonoranian in this city was killed by a native Californian. This makes eleven murders that have been perpetuated in this vicinity within the last three months and a few days. From murders to murderers the transition to the jail is easy. A few nights since no less than twelve prisoners escaped; making the third general jail delivery we have had within the last two months. Among the prisoners who have escaped are several of the most desperate criminals in existence; three of those concerned in the murder of Callahan, for instance. Another was under sentence for five years in the State Prison, for stealing horses. This is a bad state of things, all must admit, and is to be attributed to the want of energy on the part of our county court. There is no jail here but an old building erected by Col. Stevenson as a guard house, and is not at all suitable to keep criminals in; yet the authorities have made no provision for the erection of any other; and have not raised sufficient taxes to pay one half of the ordinary expenses of the county. These are much enhanced for the want of a suitable place to keep prisoners; as the expense of guarding the building in which they have been put is never less than twelve dollars a day, and has been as high as forty dollars, and yet the prisoners all manage to escape.

The jail, somehow or other, suggests Gen. Morehead. This worthy is said to have been ordered on a court martial by Gen. Bean, at San Diego. I do not understand how this can be, as there are not militia officers enough in this part of the State to form a court; but I suppose it is intended to send to the North for them, in which case there will be another fine bill to pay for somebody. Many of Morehead's men, it is said, have "broke for the mines." Others are going North with him to San José, there to be "mustered out of service."

There is a report that the Indians at the Colorado have come down upon the ferrymen and killed them all. This is not improbable, for there were but seven men there when Morehead left the river, and if it required of Morehead 130 men to kill a couple of dozen Indians, one would hardly think seven were safe after his party had retired to the settlements. Major Heintzleman has gone to the river, but was not expected to arrive until about two weeks from the time of Morehead's departure.

Daily Alta California, January 21, 1851
Our Indian Relations

The bickerings between the Indians and whites, which at first, with an ordinary degree of tact and ability, tempered with justice, might have been silenced, and subsequent difficulties been avoided, have at length reached a point when very effective measures must be pursued, or the districts bordering upon the range of the mountain tribes be, if not depopulated, at least most ruinously checked in their progress. There is no doubt that the mountain tribes have at length assumed a hostile position, and are in sufficient numbers to keep at bay any weak parties of our people who may march against them. Being thoroughly acquainted with the mountain passes, they possess great advantages over most of the whites who are disposed to take part in the foray against them. Hunger and desperation are not likely to make them very treatable, and we, therefore, anticipate much trouble ere the present warlike demonstrations shall be quieted.

The settlement of the whites in the plains and vallies [sic] has necessarily driven the game from the old grounds whence the Indians derived their supplies. Of course they attribute their threatened starvation to the presence of the whites, and reasoning as they have ever since our ancestors came into their country, they very naturally have come to the conclusion that if they could exterminate the whites the old condition of things would return. And that they can do so they fully believe. Meanwhile thefts and robberies have been committed by them and retaliations have followed. They have stolen horses and mules for food, the latter being considered by them most excellent. Thus things have been progressing until the attack upon and plundering of Savage's store and the murder of three of the four persons who were present. Since then, Savage having not met with success in his call upon the Governor for power to enlist volunteers, raised what men he could and gave battle, killing some thirty of the Indians. We have conversed with Judge Marvin, recently elected Superintendent of Public Instruction, and from him have learned many important particulars.

He represents the Indians as numbering probably seven thousand, with hostile determinations, spread through the mountains between the waters of the Tuolumne and the head waters of the San Joaquin. They have intercommunications throughout the mountain passes, by which they will probably be able to concentrate the greater part of their force upon whatever point may be attacked by the Americans. Judge Marvin's opinion is that the Indians must be pretty severely drubbed before they will so far respect our power as to keep any treaties they may agree to, if such can be entered into with them.

One thing is very evident; there must be immediate action. Our commissioners must be active, or a long, bloody and costly war is inevitable. While we hesitate or lose time, the golden moment for pacification may forever be lost. Even since this article was commenced, news has arrived of another battle, the particulars of which the reader will find in another place.

There can be no doubt that the Indian tribes of the mountains have been under-estimated by writers and others. The gentlemen above referred to says that he considers them as brave as the Mohawks or any other of the eastern tribes. It is truly lamentable that the U.S. government did not one year ago send out Commissioners to treat with them, authorised [sic] to purchase extinguishment [sic] of their titles to the land and agree upon annual subsidies sufficient to compensate them for the relinquishment of their lands, fisheries, &c. Had this been done, the Commissioner, by a judicious distribution of presents and punctual payment of all things promised, would undoubtedly have found little difficulty in placing the relation between the two races upon such a basis as would have been for the advantage of both. It looks now very doubtful whether the gentlemen of the commission will be able to secure peace before a severe lesson shall have been taught these belligerent tribes.

One of them was to leave last evening for Sonoma, to make a requisition for an escort of troops. They wish to try peaceable measures if they be practicable. It might be the wisest course to forward all the available force of the U.S. troops in the region of the difficulties, not so near as to prevent the appearance of peaceable intentions and measures on the part of the commission, which might prevent success; nor yet so far removed as to cause the loss of much time and advantageous opportunities in case the sword and the rifle alone have to become the agents of peace. We believe the commission fully competent with the aid of gentlemen well acquainted with the Indian character, who are ready to co-operate to settle the whole matter if it be possible without the last appeal. But if that be done it must be done quickly. The Saxon blood is up. and when it is so, like the rolling Mississippi, no slight levee will stay it within its channels.

Daily Alta California, February 18, 1851

If some gifted seer in these latter days could stand upon the hill of time and take a glance over a few years space into that boundless ocean whose waves will lash forever, he would behold a bright vision of California as she shall be. When we remember that but five years ago the great and flourishing State in which we now live, with the comforts and luxuries of life about us, was the grazing-ground of herds of cattle, that the immense range of mining country was the habitation of the wild Indian, that our noble bay was a mere water-ing-place for whaling vessels, and that our hills, now covered with buildings, were green with their native oak, the mind is lost in wonder and astonish-ment that in so short a space of time such a change could have been wrought.

God has given us in California a goodly heritage—a land o'er who rugged mountain sides and smiling river banks He has scattered, with a profusion rich as the bounties of His Providence, the bright sparkling gold—a land containing caves of treasure in which the lamp of Aladdin would have dimmed with the surrounding brightness—a land of broad prairies, covered with evergreen oaks, of noble hills and verdant valleys, rich with a virgin soil as yet unturned by the plough-share of the husbandman—a land blessed with a climate unexcelled almost in salubrity and a location on the face of the earth unsurpassed as the place for the *entre-pot* for the riches of the Indies, the whole eastern continent and the islands of the western seas.

However, rapid then may have been the former strides of California, it must be evident that from her great capacities, her future must be even greater than her past. Her commercial intercourse-will soon be enlarged by a steam communication between San Francisco and China, and the long and tedious voyage around either cape will be shortened. Steamboats are daily arriving which will navigate every river and navigate stream within our bor-ders—already railroads are projected, and soon we shall hear the shrill neigh of the fire-steed as he paws the ground and rushes lightning-like over the plains and through the hills. Our cities are growing with a rapidity unequaled in the history of the world. Towns are springing up in every eligible location, and permanent settlers are building up their homes amongst us. Companies are forming to work our extensive mines of silver, gold, and quicksilver, who will necessarily develop new resources, and discover new mineral wealth. Agriculturalists are turning up our virgin soil, and fields of waving grain are tossing their yellow heads in the former home of the untutored Indian. Schools are springing up and the benefits of education are extending throughout our States. Our population is fast becoming a permanent one, and with the well known energy and enterprise of the Anglo-Saxon race, California with her noble resources must inevitably become of the most pow-erful, rich and happy territories in the world.

A lofty destiny is before us, and however the clouds may sometimes lower, it is well to recollect that the faithful eye sees through the cloud, and views the blue heaven and the glorious sun which shall melt away the cloud, and leave all clear and beautiful.

Sacramento Union, November 5, 1851

Dr. Harkness informs us that a brother of his, who has just come down from the Upper Sacramento, brings intelligence that sickness prevails to a considerable extent among the tribes of Indians in the vicinity of the river. He noticed on the road a number of unburied bodies, and in the huts and woods many who were lying prostrate with disease. The ranks of the aborigines are rapidly wasting away before the onward march of the pale face; and very soon, the last son of the forest will have been summoned to the presence of "The Great Father." (As quoted in *They Were Only Diggers*, pp. 105–6.)

Sacramento Union, November 14, 1851

An Indian was murdered in Santa Barbara recently under circumstances which call loudly for the establishment of a Vigilance Committee in that place. He was called from his house by a Sonorian, whose name we did not learn, and who without any provocation whatever, plunged a knife into his heart, killing him instantly. Some four or five Indians were present, witnesses to the transaction, and they pursued the murderer, caught him and carried him before a magistrate. Will it be believed that he was almost immediately released from custody, because our laws will not allow an Indian to testify against a white man? The Indians in this part of the State, in the main a harmless race, are left entirely at the mercy of every ruffian in the country, and if something is not done for their protection, the race will shortly become extinct. (As quoted in *They Were Only Diggers*, pp. 105–6.)

From San Diego
Atrocious Murder-City Gas Contract
SAN DIEGO, Jan. 14, 1853

EDITORS ALTA: A murder of an atrocious character was perpetrated by some persons, probably Indians, in this city, during the past night. An inoffensive though dissipated old tailor, named George Warren, formerly a sergeant of the N.Y. regiment of volunteers, arrived here last evening from Los Angeles. He was seen during the evening in the various billiard rooms and other places of public resort in a state of intoxication, and early this morning an Indian in charge of some sheep in the vicinity came in and reported that his body was lying in a ravine about a quarter of a mile from the Plaza. On to the spot, he was found stripped nearly naked, his clothes having been hastily concealed beneath a bush hard by, and his brains literally beaten out. A jaw bone of an ox laid near him covered with blood, brains and mangled masses of flesh and hair. He was at once removed to the City Hall and a coroner's jury was assembled, in whose presence a post examination is now being conducted. Suspicion points to certain Indians last seen in his company, who undoubtedly murdered the poor wretch for the sake of the miserable clothing he wore.

Our city is infested with a gang of Indian thieves and murderers, who should be driven out or brought to condign punishment.

It is the intention of our worthy Justice of Peace, Judge Franklin, to spare no efforts to discover the perpetrators of this foul and inhuman [*sic*] murder, and we trust he may prove successful in his endeavors.

Daily Alta California, March 27, 1853

Allen Penrod, a worthy citizen of Jackson county, Illinois, was murdered by the Indians on the 23d instant, while at work on his claim at Dark Canon.

Daily Alta California, April 1, 1853
Sonora Correspondence
The Rain—Rivers in the South Rising—Murder by the Indians—
Very Rich Diggings
SONORA, March 28th, 1853

The rain which began yesterday still continues with unabated violence. It is a very warm rain, and has melted the snow in the mountains so that the rivers have been very sensibly affected. The Stanislaus, I am informed, had risen at 4 o'clock this afternoon some 6 or 8 feet, and was rapidly getting higher.

A Mr. Slater, who has had a ranch in the vicinity of Dodge's, some five miles from Sonora, was found murdered yesterday, and his body much eaten by wolves. The head, arms and legs had been carried away, and not enough left to identify him, had he not been previously missed. At the time he was killed he was going to his work alone, with his axe, and was not found for several days. It was supposed that the deed was done by the Indians, as they are continually committing depredations in the neighborhood. A man named Stanley was killed near there a few weeks ago.

Very rich diggings have lately been discovered at Poverty hill. The lead is said to be very extensive and deep. It runs along the side of a hill apparently for nearly half a mile, and all the claims that have been drifted in far enough have struck it very rich. As high as two ounces to the pan has been taken out, or $500 a day to four hands. Despite the forbidding name of this place, it is said the diggings are rich and extensive. The Hydraulic Race is completed to this place and no lack of water is again anticipated for a long time.

PEREGRINE PILGRIM.

Daily Alta California, April 18, 1853

BODIES FOUND. The discovery of two bodies, bearing marks of foul play having been resorted to in their capture, were found near San Antonio Creek a few days since. They were Mexicans or Chileans, and seemed to have met their death from blows inflicted by an axe [sic]. Supposed to have been murdered by the Indians.

Daily Alta California, April 22, 1853
From Shasta and the Northern Mines

The first copy of the Shasta newspaper that we have seen for several weeks was handed to us Tuesday evening. We find the following items in the *Courier.*

LARGE GATHERING OF FRIENDLY INDIANS—A company of from 800 to 1000 Indians assembled in One Horsetown in Monday night last, for the purpose of celebrating the anniversary of some noted event in their history. They were painted and dressed in every conceivable fashion of the fantastic and horrible, and danced and howled, and otherwise made night hideous, for some six or eight hours "by Shrewsbury clock." After which the squaws indulged in a sumptuous repast of broiled beef guts, and the warriors partook heartily of an abundant lay-out of *shemuck*, composed of pulverized acorns, grass seed and preserved worms. They then good-humoredly retired to their peaceful holes in the valleys that they love, away up in the hills. *Hi U* Indians

AN INDIAN THIEF KILLED BY ORDER OF HIS CHIEF.—A few days ago, one of the Cow Creek Indians stole some property from one of the ranch men near Cow Creek. As soon as his chief, Numtarimon, ascertained the fact, he, with some of his men, started in pursuit of the offender, and caught him a short distance above Woodman's Ranch. While returning to the ranch the thief endeavored to make his escape, when, by order of Numtarimon, he was shot dead with arrows. This is one of the good results of a stern policy toward Indians. It has cowed that tribe; they fear the whites. Numtarimon sees the speedy and utter annihilation of his tribe, unless they will live on terms of friendship with the whites. Hence, and it is the only reason, he does all that one man can do to keep his men from stealing stock from the whites. Numtarimon is what we call "much good Indian"—that is, an Indian who refrains from stealing through fear.

Daily Alta California, June 13, 1853
Monterey, June 6, 1853

Sir: The few remaining Indians in Carmel Valley are supposed to be the remnant of the tribe that originally inhabited the place, previous to the founding of the mission in 1767, all the others having returned to their homes in the Tulare Valley and Sierra Nevada at the time the missions were secularized by the Mexican Congress in 1834, "which act," says Maj. McKinstry, "ruined forever the most successful and splendid attempt the world has ever seen made for the civilization of savage tribes." The Carmel Indians claim to be the descendants of a race once superior to all others in California, and although they are now perhaps the most degraded, from the too free use of *fire water,* yet they bear the indelible stamp of supremacy in rank and intelligence, compared with the Diggers of the Tulares. They are the only Indians in this country who appear to have legends and traditions. These tribes are classified and kept distinct. Like the Mandans, Iroquois and Shoshones, their hereditary pride has preserved all that stoicism of savage credulity in regard to effects, the cause of which they could not understand; and their *medicine men* were ever ready to weave some absurd legend, discovering here and there a grain of truth on its surface—all, however, stamped with that freedom of though, bold conception, and laconic style of narrative so characteristic of savage life in all countries, and particularly of the native Americans.

In the fall of 1852, died at the rancheria of his tribe, in Carmel, an Indian supposed to be one hundred and forty old. An old settler in Monterey informed me that the Indian was baptized in 1776, and was then, as is shown by the register of baptism at San Carlos, an old man. In the spring of 1847, I first saw him; he was then blind, and had been so, I was informed, over forty years; his toes and fingers were hard as a piece of horn; in fact, the whole foot appeared as if it was petrified. He was well known by most of the citizens of Monterey, his family deriving a handsome revenue from the liberality of visitors, who familiarly termed him "Old Uncle Ned." In his family is a tradition, as related to me by Capt. Maryatt, an old California hunter and trapper, which appears to have had its origin in truth.

There is no doubt that the present Bay of Carmel was once the mouth of an active volcano, as the remains of lava and the piles of vitrified rock amply testify. The rocks in the vicinity of San Antonio, as well as those near Pechezo's Peak, bear the same indications of volcanic action, nor is Monte Diablo an exception, nor any part of the Sierra Nevada. The geologist who can trace causes from effects would at once pronounce the Bay of San

Francisco of recent formation. The appearance of the [illegible] or Golden Gate, and the rocks, trees and soil of the surrounding country, argue the correctness of the theory. Another proof is in the fact that there is not to be found in any of the gold region, fossil remains of marine shells and animals. The scarcity of timber in the great vallies [sic] of the interior would seem to indicate that they were, at no distant period, covered with water.

It takes but a little stretch of the imagination to refer back to the time when these vallies [sic], like our western lakes, stretched their broad and expansive wings from mountain to mountain, while, like sentinels, many a miniature Vesuvius and Ætna loomed up, a fountain of fire before the tiny fleet of a people who, like those lakes and those beacons, have passed away. There is no doubt that volcanic action flooded these plains with salt water from the ocean, as there are remains of marine shells; etc., almost perfect, to be found in many places near the Tule Lakes. The exploring party of 1849, near the slough that intersects Buena Vista with Kern Lake, discovered the large neck or fin bone of a whale together with several of the ribs. My informant, who had seen numerous similar remains on the beach at Monterey, told me they were in a good state of preservation, and that he had also seen the shells of muscles [sic] and *abalones*, almost as perfect as those we were digging up, near the beach, to burn into lime.

In my next I shall give the legend of the gold region, and in one time should it prove acceptable to your readers, two other legends, as well as some "camp yarns" that were current among the early hunters and trappers of the Northwest Fur Company in California, with some of the scrapes and sprees of said Capt. Maryatt, (related in his own peculiar style), while he was "whipperin" to some Spang-yang-yan-yards in the ken-yen-yons of the Sag-a-rag-a-ra-mento.

DON K.

Sacramento Union, February 3, 1855
Indian War

The accounts from the North indicate the commencement of a war of extermination against the Indians. The latter commenced the attack of the Klamath; but who can determine their provocation or the amount of destitution suffered before the hostile blow was struck.

The intrusion of the white man upon the Indian's hunting grounds has driven off the game and destroyed their fisheries. The consequence is, the Indians suffer every winter for sustenance. Hunger and starvation follows them wherever they go. Is it, then, a matter of wonder that they become desperate and resort to stealing and killing? They are driven to steal or starve, and the Indian mode is to kill and then plunder.

The policy of our Government towards the Indians in this State is most miserable. Had reasonable care been exercised to see that they were provided with something to eat and wear in this State, no necessity would have presented itself for an indiscriminate slaughter of the race.

The fate of the Indian is fixed. He must be annihilated by the advance of the white man; by the disease, and, to them, the evils of civilization. But the work should not have been commenced at so early a day by the deadly rifle.

To show how the matter is viewed on the Klamath, we copy the following from the Crescent City *Herald*. The people look upon it there as a war of extermination, and are killing all grown up males. A writer from Trinidad, under date of January 22d, says:

I shall start the two Indians that came down with me tonight, and hope they may reach Crescent City in safety, although I think it exceedingly doubtful, as the whites are shooting them whenever an opportunity offers; for this reason I start them in the night, hoping they may be out of danger ere morning. On the Klamath the Indians have killed six white men, and I understand some stock. From the Salmon down the whites are in arms, with determination, I believe if possible, to destroy all the grown up males, notwithstanding this meets with the opposition of some few who have favorite Indians amongst them. I doubt whether this discrimination should be made, as some who have been considered good have proved the most treacherous. I understand that the ferry of Mr. Boyce, as also that of Mr. Simms, has been cut away. Messrs. Norton and Beard have moved their families from Elk Camp to Trinidad; they were the only white females in that section that were exposed to the savages. I have no doubt there will be warm times on the Klamath for some weeks, as the Indians are numerous, well armed and determined to fight. (As quoted in *The Destruction of California Indians*, pp. 35-36.)

San Francisco Bulletin, September 23, 1858
Condition of the Indians in Tuolomne County

The Tuolomne *Courier* draws the following picture of the miserable condition of the Indians in and about Columbia:

For months past our feelings have been shocked at the condition of the Indians who are located about this neighborhood. There is no sympathizing care extended to these frail relics of humanity, as the storms sweep over their miserable huts and unclad bodies. Their intercourse with civilized communities has been accompanied with the ordinary results which other tribes have experienced under similar circumstances: prostitution, intemperance, and vice, in their most revolting aspects. As soon as the grey light of morning appears, they may be seen prowling round in search of miserable offal, for which they must compete with the dogs. At midnight their savage howls may frequently be heard, as they return to their sleeping places, half crazy from the poisonous drink which they have imbibed from some of the low grogeries about the outskirts of the town. A few weeks ago, one of their number murdered another in the vicinity of the Catholic church, while raving with madness from the above cause. But there is no law enforced for these poor wretches. It is no one's business to look after and to protect them. Why do not our citizens ask the Legislature to have them removed to one of the reservations, where they will be comfortable, and be afforded an opportunity of learning some of the Christian ways of civilized beings? (As quoted in *The Destruction of California Indians*, p. 37.)

San Joaquin Republican, September, 1858

The Fresno Indians, says the *San Joaquin Republican* (Sept. 1858) are killing their doctors or medicine-men. They declare them to be witches, that they cannot cure the sick, and that there will be no more rain or green grass until they are exterminated. Seven or eight of their doctors have in consequence already suffered martyrdom. One of the survivors came running into the camp of Mr. Ridgway, on the Fresno, and asked protection. He was pursued by some sixteen Indians, who demanded him of Mr. Ridgway, and gave the above reason why they ought to have him. Their modest request was refused, but a few days afterwards the doctor ventured out and they got him. (As quoted in *They Were Only Diggers*, pp. 113-14.)

San Francisco Bulletin, September 1, 1856
Indian Affairs on the Pacific

For a long time past, and indeed throughout the whole of the continuance of the war with the Indians that has existed in Washington Territory, Oregon, and the northern part of this State, the papers published in those neighborhoods have teemed with strictures upon the course pursued by the officers in command of the U.S. troops, and strong condemnation of the policy by which they appear to have been governed. The Executive officers of each of those Territories have echoed the sentiments expressed in the papers, and have made severe charges against the government officers who were sent against the Indians. When the Regulars and the Volunteers were in the field together, it seemed almost impossible to get them to act in concert, and indeed they were occasionally almost opposed to each other. This state of things is the natural result of the pursuance by the officers of the U.S. Government, and the settlers and frontiersmen, of two lines of policy which are directly opposed to each other—the one, the policy of protection; the other, that of extermination. Indian affairs upon the Pacific coast have come to such a pass, that for the maintenance of peace in our borders, one policy or the other must be at once adopted and adhered to. Extermination is the quickest and cheapest remedy, and effectually prevents all after difficulty when an outbreak occurs. But that civilized men, and Americans at that, can be found to openly propose and advocate such a remedy, is disgraceful to our nation, whether we look only to the barbarity of the measure, or the neglect of the general government, which has permitted matters to get into such a state as even apparently to justify such a recommendation, or the adoption of such measures as would carry it into effect.

The policy of the government of the United States when sincerely acted upon and carried out is really benevolent, and the desire of those having the direction of Indian affairs at Washington, is ostensibly to protect the Indians, and assist and encourage them while accustoming themselves to the new habits and modes of living which are forced upon them by the continual and rapid encroachments of their white neighbors upon their ancient hunting grounds. But while such feelings may influence the authorities at Washington, and even govern the actions of all honest agents of the government who deal directly with the Indians, a very different sort of desires appear to influence a large portion of the inhabitants of our border districts. With them every inconvenience the result of the contact of the two races is to be remedied only by driving the red men back or by their extermination.

We are told that the Indians are treacherous, that it is impossible for white men to live in safety while Indians remain in the neighborhood; that the whites are continually exposed to sudden and unexpected outbreaks on the part of the Indians, for which it is impossible to be prepared and fully to run the risk of. Therefore, it is necessary for the whites to rid themselves of the presence of the Indians. If they refuse to move upon the demand of the settlers, a relentless course of punishment for the most trivial offences [sic] is adopted, which is putting into operation without a declaration of war, the policy of extermination. A single instance in point, that occurred several years ago, in one of the northern counties of this State, may be given to illustrate the utter disregard of the lives of these human beings that exists in the breasts in many of the class of whom we speak. The Indians near a small mining camp, having discovered that one of the miners left his bowl of sugar upon a shelf directly under the canvass roof of his cabin, cut a hole in it and helped themselves to a pound or so of sugar, two or three times. The miner, who had a medicine chest with him, took an ounce of strychnine that was in it, and, mixing it with a larger quantity of sugar than usual, filled the bowl with it, and placing it in its former position went to his work. The Indians taking it again, as before, and, making somewhat of a feast with it, the result was that some eight or ten were killed outright, and as many more only recovered after suffering severely. What plea can be urged to justify such an act as that? And yet though this act alone is enough to inspire horror, it is but one of many equally atrocious. The same principle has been and is yet carried out in nearly all the dealings of the white men with Indians. It is the cruel and extreme punishment of small offences, when committed by the Indians, death being made to follow the slightest transgression, when light or trifling penalties only would have been visited upon the culprit had he been an American or other white man.

When life is taken in this way, is it wonderful if savages, the relatives of those who are killed, endeavor to revenge themselves? And is it surprising if the Indians, feeling their inability to cope with the white man openly, yet burning of revenge, seek it stealthily, and by assassination of single individuals? Is it wonderful that in seeking it thus they frequently take, by accident or purposely, the life of persons who have not injured them? In revenging injuries upon them have the whites always been particular in finding the precise culprit and punished him only? He is little conversant with the history of Indian affairs in this State who cannot call to mind instances where, when one or two white men had been found killed by Indians, (whether in defence [sic] of life itself, or their dearest rights, inquiry never being made) to revenge them, all the inhabitants of a rancheria or village, young and old—men, women and children, were put to death.

If one white man, no matter how worthless he may be, nor how deserving of death, be killed by Indians, it is published in every paper in the State, and revenge is loudly called for. But the Indians have no newspapers. They may suffer every wrong it is possible to heap upon an injured and oppressed people, and if it is done out of our cities or villages, and out of the sight of any save the wrong doers, the world may never hear of it. They have no newspapers, and few indeed are their friends and those who are willing to speak for them.

The facts bear us out in asserting, and it is apparent to every one who has ever lived in the mountains of the State, that white men by their oppression of, and injustice to, the Indians, have been the means of bringing upon their fellows, and upon the innocent wives and children of unoffending settlers, all the horrors of Indian hostilities in almost every instance in which they have broken out on the Pacific border. We shall consider the subject further and speak of the remedy. (As quoted in *The Destruction of California Indians*, pp. 205-8.)

San Francisco Bulletin, October 27, 1858
Indians of the Shasta and Scott Valleys

George W. Taylor writes a letter to the Yreka Union, complaining of the manner in which the remnant of the Shasta and Scott Indians has been treated by the Government. He says that these Indians some time ago assembled at Fort Jones, Scott Valley, and gave up their arms on a promise of the United States of protection and support. From that time till about three months ago, these Indians have remained peaceable and quiet; and have been regularly supplied with food from the fort; as per agreement. About three months ago, this fort was abandoned; and some sixty or seventy Indians are thus left entirely destitute of adequate means of berries, fishing and stealing. Mr. [Taylor] thus exposes the meagre nature of these resources:

As to hunting, if they had arms and ammunition they could obtain but a meagre supply, as nearly all the game has been driven off their hunting grounds by the whites, and they are too weak to trespass with impunity upon the hunting grounds of their neighbors. As to fishing, owing to the obstructions in the river, for which the Indians are not accountable, but few fish have made their appearance this high up the stream; and as for berries suitable for the food of man, they are like "angel's visits" as far as this region is concerned. The winter is at hand, and then the poor Indian has no other resource than to beg, steal or starve; and who doubts or can blame them for the result, if driven to extremities. We all know they will steal, and murder too, if necessary, to supply the wants of nature; and will they not be justified in so doing? Necessity knows no law; and was a maxim in jurisprudence, as long ago as the days of Solon and Lycurgus, and it is one of the few rules to which there is no exception.

I am informed that the U.S. officers at Fort Crook, in Pitt river valley, are issuing four hundred rations daily to the Pitt river Indians, and they certainly have far less claims upon the government for aid and support, than have the Indians of Shasta and Scott valleys.

It is suggested to call a meeting of the citizens of the Yreka to petition the Indian Agent to extend some kind of relief to these starving savages.

Nevada National, October, 1858

Recently, a grand Digger jollification was held near Barker's ranch, Nevada county. There were about 150 Indians—men, women and children—present, although only about fifty warriors engaged in active operations. The *Nevada National* of October 1858 thus describes the performance of the War Dance by the braves:

Each warrior held his bow and quiver of arrows in his hand, and each one had two and sometimes three whistles, made of reeds, in his mouth. With these primitive whistles they produced a monotonous but not unpleasant cadence, to which they kept time with their feet. They were mostly naked to their waists, and their faces and bodies were painted either bright vermilion, striped with fanciful figures of charcoal, or with a reddish brown paint. However, two or three, disdaining innovations upon their national costume, wore Adam's livery, with a breech-cloth, and represent the old arch-enemy of man himself. Each one wore a head-dress of feathers and beads, and a turban of skins. After numerous gyrations indescribable, they would suddenly stop with a yell that made the mountain echoes ring, and it seemed to be a point with them that he who did not stop on the instant was the butt of laughter, and the jest of the crowd. In the back ground their bush tents were arranged, where the women and children were spectators, for it is the Digger custom that the sexes do not amalgamate in their festivities; and when the men dance the other sex do not join, and when the women have a jollification the men are spectators. (As quoted in *They Were Only Diggers*, p. 114.)

★★

Chapter 2

NATIVE AMERICAN REACTION TO THE INVASION

W ith the coming of the Gold Rush, thousands of non-Indians converged on California in hope of becoming wealthy. They established mining camps in the Sierra Nevada Mountains and erected communities throughout what became the Golden State. This constituted an invasion, for these outsiders entered the homelands of numerous Native American peoples without their consent. Anglos, Englishmen, Germans, Chileans, Chinese, Mexicans, and others moved into areas already occupied by Indians. Foreigners came to take, to rob the region of its mineral wealth. They viewed the indigenous inhabitants of California as obstructing their ability to mine gold.

Miners likely did not reflect on the impact of their incursion into California. They polluted rivers and streams, killed local game, destroyed plant habitats, and upset the lives of thousands of Native Americans. Prospectors frequently attempted to force Indians off their native lands so that they could search for gold. During the 1850s and 1860s, the United States government sought to place some indigenous peoples of California onto reservations and teach them Christianity and American farming techniques. Others the government ignored, allowing state officials and local law informants to establish rule over Indians. Miners, immigrants, and government officials oppressed the original inhabitants of the Golden State.

Despite overwhelming numbers of invaders, Native Americans in California resisted. They strived to continue their traditional lifestyles, yet expediency demanded that they also mobilize. After the Spanish intrusion, California Indians became increasingly warlike in order to preserve and protect themselves, their families, and their cultures. By the Gold Rush era, some Native Americans in California were adroit raiders. They successfully seized horses, livestock, and supplies from miners, ranchers, and immigrants in order to survive. With the depletion of traditional game, Indians had no other alternative but to steal from non-Indians.

The following documents reveal the effectiveness of native raids on Americans and other foreigners. Indians from all parts of the Golden State, as well as from Utah and Arizona, conducted such campaigns quickly and effectively. In this manner, Native Americans manifested their displeasure regarding the invasion of their lands. A few of the articles also focus on the Glanton killings on the Colorado River, when [Quechans] sought reprisals against a gang of outlaws.

Daily Alta California, January 8, 1851

You are doubtless aware that, early last winter, a company of American outlaws stationed themselves at the crossing of the Colorado, immediately at the mouth of the Gila and established a ferry over that great thoroughfare. Its leader, John Glanton, formerly of Texas, was a man of the most desperate character, and if report does not do them injustice, his associates were not a great deal better. Glanton had killed several men before he left San Antonio, his former place of residence. Coming into Chihuahua, he engaged in the service of that government in the delectable employment of killing Apaches, at so much per head. Finding it not to pay as well as he expected, and coming into contact with some Mexicans, whose tonsil [tousle] appearance resembled Indians, he coolly despatched [sic] them, and brought their scalps to his Excellency the Governor, and received from him for the murder of his own countrymen, the standard *pro rata* for killing Indians as far as Glanton was concerned. The atmosphere of Chihuahua became uncomfortable.

Its government finally offered a reward of $8000 for his head, an act which at least showed how much higher it estimated the head of an American than it did that of an Apache, the highest price paid for the latter being but $250. Upon this Glanton and his party "sloped," and the next we hear of him is in connection with a Dr. Lincoln and his party at the river Colorado, engaged in crossing over its turbid waters the Sonoranian Hordes, whose presence in the southern mines this summer has been the cause of so much excitement and bloodshed. But Dr. Lincoln's previous history is equally pertinent of remark with Capt. Glanton's and partially is a fault which, as a historian, I am most anxious to avoid. Dr. L. was we believe a native of Tennessee, but previous to his leaving for this country he had been residing for several years at Shreveport, on the Red River in Louisiana. On his way hither he became "flat broke," and he threw himself upon the hospitality of one who to the knowledge of the writer, is a very intelligent and excellent man, Mr. J. P. Brodie, *adminstrador* of a cotton factory in the vicinity of San Miguel, in the state of Sonora. He soon succeeded in ingratiating himself into the favor of Mr. Brodie, who fitted him out with a sufficiency to enable him to establish a ferry at the mouth of the Gila, for which it was agreed that one half of the nett [*sic*] proceeds should accrue to his (B.'s) benefit.

Your readers have by this time, Mr. Editor, learned sufficient of Dr. Lincoln's biography. We next find him and his party at the mouth of the Gila engaged in constructing an adobe house, boats, &c., while preparatory to commencing his ferry operations. While thus employed, Glanton made his appearance, and it was soon determined that the two parties should unite and divide the profits. Glanton was elected captain of the gang. The profits of the ferry, thus established was most enormous. The throng of Mexicans that passed it the last season was supposed to exceed thirty thousand, and the charges imposed upon them by the ferry company was said to be extortionate. About the 1st of April last, Gen. Anderson, of Tennessee, came through with a party of Americans, and not relishing Glanton's charges, went to work and constructed a boat for himself, and then ferried over his company, much to the annoyance of the patriots at the mouth of the Gila. But the worst of it was, that on leaving the river, he presented his boat to the Indians, who commenced the business of ferrying on their own account at the "Algodones." This was a serious matter to Glanton and his party, and they at once proceeded to put a stop to it. Glanton took a few men, and marched down to the Indian ferry, seized their boat and destroyed it, and not content with this, took on an Irishman, whom the Indians had enlisted in their service, tied his hands and heels together, and threw him into the Colorado. This conduct, as a matter of course, at once aroused the hostility of the Indians, but the old chief, with a magnanimity and a forbearance which his more savage neighbors would have done well to have imitated, took occasion to visit Glanton and his party to expostulate with them upon their conduct. On returning to his village he called together his braves, and it was by them determined that the Americans must die.

Before this resolution of the Indians could be carried into effect, Glanton, with a few men, left on a visit to San Diego, and the Indians determined to suspend their fell design until his return. Upon this visit Glanton took with him a considerable sum of money, and deposited with Judge Hays of that place some $8,000, which still remains to his credit in the hands of that functionary. During this visit, one of his men, Brown by name, having had a few words of altercation with a soldier at San Diego, took out a revolver and deliberately shot him through. Brown was arrested and placed under guard, there being no jail in San Diego; but having been furnished with money by Glanton, he made an arrangement with the guard to be released upon payment of $500. He and the guard were to escape together. But him [he] of the sentry got into a worse box than ever he did before. The moment Brown got him out of the precincts of the town, he presented a revolver at his breast, and told him if he did not fork over the $500 he would serve him as he had served his comrade. Of course the $500 was forthcoming in a twinkling. Brown escaped, and went to the north, but afterwards, as he tells me, at the solicitations of Gov. Burnett, he came down as a guide for Gen. Morehead. But he found on getting here that the authorities of San Diego had offered a reward of several hundred dollars for his arrest, and in disgust he concluded to decline a military employment and devote his talents to a civic career.

He is now the principal deputy of the Sheriff of the County of Los Angeles. The course of events has led me a long chase away from Capt. Glanton, and I must now return with him to the Rio Colorado.

It was on the morning of the 21st of April last, that Glanton and his party reached the camp of their association at the mouth of the Gila. The day being quite warm, he, with several others, lay down to rest, and were soon in a profound slumber. The camp they occupied was covered with bushes at the top but open at the sides. The Houmas [sic] were scattered all about, and never appeared more sociable and friendly. But the hatred of an Indian never slumbers. Their arrangements had been well taken. A chosen band of the strongest nerved warriors were in attendance with stout clubs prepared for the occasion, and at an opportune moment the signal was given. Glanton was struck while asleep, but with the ready instinct of habit, he half rose and placed his hand upon his revolver. But his hour had come. A well directed blow from the stalwart arm of *Cavallo sin Palo* [sic], (horse without hair,) "did his business." He was in the land that is never re-visited. The fate which he had so often meted out to others, it appears had been reserved for himself. Dr. Lincoln, it is said, was one of the few that detected the movement of the Indians just as they made their attack. He defended himself with desperation, but in less than three minutes every individual belonging to the ferry company, then present, had ceased to breathe. Their mangled remains were thrown into a pile of combustibles and burned; their bones can be seen there to this day. Three of Glanton's party were distant from the camp about half a mile. Several of the Indians were despatched [sic] to kill these at the same time the massacre of their companions was to take place, but these men were too sharp for them. From the movements of the Indians their suspicions were excited and they rushed for the river. A shower of arrows, and not a few firearms saluted them as they passed the camp, but they managed to get to a small boat and escape down the river, from whence they reached a company of Mexicans, and in this way arrived at the settlements. Thus terminated the movements of Capt. Glanton and Dr. Lincoln, but their deaths was the commencement of a series of measures whose end is not yet, and additional space to develop. I will only here add furthermore, that there were present as witnesses to the murder of Glanton and his party, a large company of Mexicans, who either did not dare, or did not choose to interfere. The account I have given was related by one of the chiefs engaged in it. The Indians are by no means reserved upon the subject, but dwell upon their feats of strength with infinite gusto.

Adios, THEODORO.

Daily Alta California, January 14, 1851
Los Angeles Correspondence

The letter of our correspondent, "Theodoro," giving a detailed account of the massacre of Glanton and his party, and the circumstances which led to it were published in the *Alta* of the 8th inst. The following, which has been deferred for want of room is the commencement of a history of Gen. Morehead.

The news of the murder of Glanton and his companions as it reached the settlements, occasioned as may be supposed, no little excitement. It was not, however, so much from any particular sympathy for the fate of the men who had been slaughtered that public feeling was aroused, for their character was pretty well understood, but it was from the fact that there was known to be at this time several companies of American immigrants descending the Gila and it was thought doubtful as to the treatment they might receive at the hands of the Indians these last having just had a lap of American blood. Furthermore, the season for the spring immigration from the states by the lower routes was near at hand, and it was thought highly important that something should be done by government for its protection at the crossing of the Colorado. To this end a meeting was held in San Diego by the inhabitants, and Gen. Smith memorialized upon the subject. The citizens of Los Angeles, not being quite so public spirited as are those of its more enterprising neighbor, did not go quite so far as this, but when the three survivors of Glanton's party came up, they were induced to go before the Alcalde, Abel Stearns, Esq., and make a deposition as to the state of things at the river. Col. Magruder, who chanced at that time to be at the place, with that patriotic spirit which characterizes him, volunteered to Mr. Stearns a written guarantee that on forwarding this document to the authorities, if the expense of so doing so was not defrayed by them, he himself would pay it out of his own pocket. Upon this consideration Mr. Stearns employed a special messenger to convey the tidings to the north. At Col. Magruder's suggestion, the papers were taken before Mr. Stearns were sent Gov. Burnett, while he himself addressed Gen. Smith upon the subject. It was supposed both by Mr. Stearns and Mr. Magruder that the Governor would feel called upon to order out the militia of the state upon the occasion. But in this they were mistaken. His Excellency at once responded by directing the sheriffs of Los Angeles and San Diego counties to enlist into the service of the state sixty men, to be under the general charge of Major General Bean of San Diego, and to be by him transferred to the region of the Yumas, under the control of some trusty subaltern. Gen. Smith, as soon as he received Col. Magruder'e [sic] letter, at once commanded Major Fitzgerald to hold himself in readiness with his command to proceed to the river; so that it will be noticed that the documents forwarded by Mr. Stearns produced a much more potent effect than is usual with such applications, for they obtained not merely what was asked for, but a great deal more.

As the conduct of Gov. Burnett in regard to this affair will no doubt be closely canvassed at San Jose, the coming winter I shall here content myself with offering a very few observations respecting it. In the first place, it seems to me very doubtful as to the legal right of the Governor to call out the troops at all under the provisions, of the constitution, upon which he is presumed to have acted. Secondly: Even if there had been a formidable invasion of American soil it seems to me Gov. B. acted most imprudently in calling out the militia, until he had conferred with Gen. Smith upon the subject, for it is worthy of remark that at the very time he was calling upon the sheriffs of San Diego and Los Angeles Counties for a force of sixty men, there was at least double that number of soldiers in the immediate vicinity of San Diego, having nothing on earth to do but to keep guard over each other. Thirdly: The Governor seems to have entertained very erroneous opinions in regard to the nature increased to one hundred, and even then suggests that probably the U.S. troops will co-operate in the expedition. Now any one at all acquainted with the condition of things at the Colorado could have told him that twenty-five men would be of as much service as twenty-five hundred. But it is time to resume the thread of my story.

The orders of the Governor were made to Gen. Bean, without any allusion to the party by whom they were to be carried out. But he appears to have had a private understanding with a gentleman whose name and exploits must figure conspicuously hereafter in our narrative Gen. Morehead, as he is termed, for what reason I am unable to say, is a native of Kentucky, and is said to be a son or nephew of Gov. Morehead of that state. His first entrance into the duties of this troublesome world was as Lieutenant in Col. Stevenson's regiment of

New York volunteers, in which capacity California gained the honor of his acquaintance. He last year represented one of the mining districts in the Legislature, and is said to be the law partner of the Attorney General of this state. This is the person whom Gov. Burnett, at least unofficially, (for Morehead has not claimed to have received any directions from the Governor) appointed to head the expedition against the Yumas. With how much wisdom the reader may judge. Gen. Morehead brought with him from San Jose the orders of the Government to Gen. Bean, and at the same time some twenty men, who were to form the nucleus of the expedition.

Before leaving this part of the subject it is but an act of justice to state that the Governor, in his address to Gen. Bean, left much to his discretion, in fact he threw the whole responsibility of the affair upon him, instructing him to act according to circumstances. Furthermore, as early as the 4th of September he peremptorily ordered the expedition disbanded, and says he would have done so previously, but that he was under the impression that, owing to the difficulty of procuring men, it had never been organized.

The orders of the Governor to Gen. Bean were entirely silent upon the difficult subject of finance. Whether his Excellency supposed that the people in this region would defray the expenses of the expedition by voluntary contribution, or whether the omission was accidental, or whether, in short, he wished to evade the responsibility of the act, are points upon which the reader must exercise his own sagacity. But whatever might have been the views of the Governor, his silence upon the subject had little influence over the minds of his doughty lieutenants. Gen. Bean appears to be a soldier of the "I take the responsibility" order. He did not hesitate to meet the emergency by directing Gen. Morehead to defray the expenses of the expedition, by giving drafts in his own name, on the treasury of the State; and Gen. Morehead did not hesitate to assure the public that not only would these drafts be paid at sight, but to the rancheros in the country that they would be received in this city for taxes.

The obvious duty of Gen. Bean, on receiving the orders of the Governor, should have been, in my opinion, either to have required from his Excellency more explicit directions, or, what would have been still better, to have this, he deputes to an inexperienced person not merely the entire management of a most important enterprise but the grave power of issuing drafts upon the treasury, not only without stint or limit, but without presenting, and mode by which it can be ascertained for what purpose they were emitted, or to what end converted.

It should have been noted that Gen. Bean's orders to Gen. Morehead were dated on the 11th of July. At this time there were at the river two companies of American ferrymen, and a third was expected down from San Francisco daily. Not only this, but traveling traders were going to and returning from the Colorado occasionally, and trains of emigrants were passing and repassing that river every few days. Now, as from none of these had there been a syllable of complaint about the conduct of the Indians; and, as they were known to have committed no aggressions of consequence upon Americans since the date of Glanton's massacre, the reader will probably be a little puzzled at the necessity of the expedition at this time. But what will he say when he learns that before it finally left for the Colorado, a company had come down, and had actually gone on to the river with a view of establishing a settlement in the vicinity, so little fear had they of the Yumas, and furthermore that Maj. Heintzleman, after innumerable delays, was just upon the point of setting out to execute the orders of Gen. Smith and had actually his wagons laden with provisions upon the road.

The shrewdness of the reader has anticipated the remark that the new species of circulating medium called into being at the behest of the valiant Bean met with a very cool reception from the citizens of Los Angeles County generally. When the old rancheros were asked to part with their animals and other property for "Morehead's scrip," as it is significantly termed, they resolutely ejaculated "*No quiero*," which it is here stated, for the information of the unlettered reader means that they were not solicitous of the exchange. It is the peculiar province of great men to triumph over obstacles. Gen. Morehead affords no exception to this rule. His genius at once rose with the occasion. By dint of a little study he arrived at the conclusion that, by virtue of his commission from Gen. Bean, he was not only entitled to have his "scrip" pass current among the "masses," but that for the purposes of his expedition, he could seize animals from the rancheros, "*quiero*" or "*no quiero*." He lost no time in putting these sage conclusions into effect. Scouts, by his authority were dispatched into the country, and levies of animals made from the *caballaros* [sic] of Don Ricardo Bejor, Don Bernardo Yorba, Don Jose M. Lugo, and many others.

Daily Alta California, January 20, 1851
Gen. Morehead's Expedition

From this time scouts were sent out daily in pursuit of the Indians. Morehead himself, with his main command, crossed over the Colorado to the point of land between that river and the Gila, where the Indians have their principal settlement. The Indians, perceiving his approach, were busy in packing their little wares upon their animals, preparitory [sic] to a hasty retreat. Morehead at once commenced an attack upon them, and followed them so closely that most of them were compelled to throw away every encumberance [sic] to ensure their own safety. They were followed for many miles—several were shot, and some of their animals were taken. From this time forward, few or no Indians were seen. They retreated up to the river, leaving their crops and their possessions to the mercy of their foe. How extensive these are the reader will hardly he prepared to believe. We are assured by one who rode over the fields that they extended many miles.

All these were at once appropriated by Morehead to the purpose of his command. His animals were turned in upon them as were also those of different companies of emigrants as they came up. Not content with this, he caused the huts of the Indians to be sacked and despoiled of large quantities of musquite [sic] beans. These it is well known are a prime article of food with the Indians in this vicinity. Pounded up and mixed with stewed pumpkins they make a bread that is not only nutritious but not altogether palatable. The musquite [sic] is very prolific about the Colorado, and the Indians had stored up large quantities for the winter's consumption, but all that fell in his way were destroyed by Gen. Morehead.

Thus terminated this forray [sic] against the Indians. We shall leave the reader to draw his own conclusions upon the wisdom of the mode in which it was conducted. Two results however it seems to us must be inevitable. The first is, most extensive and severe suffering on the part of the Indians from the destruction of their crops, and the other is an ineradicable feeling of hostility will be implanted in their savage natures, which will not fail to wreak itself on every small body of emigrants that fall in their way. Fortunately for travelers the post at the mouth of the Gila is now in possession of an experienced and discreet commander, who will be able, we trust, to convince the Indians that the Americans will neither sanction robbery *from* them, nor allow it to be practised [sic] *upon* them.

Daily Alta California, February 13, 1851
Indian Expedition
STOCKTON, Feb. 11th, 1851

In this country, more than any other portion of the United States, is it difficult to fit out a military expedition for a lengthy campaign, and for that reason the expedition to treat with the Indians has not yet left. Everything is in readiness now, however, and the military encampment will be broken up to-morrow morning.

To-day Dr. Wozencroft and Col. Barbour, of the commission [sic], Judge Marvin, Superintendant [sic] of Pubic Instruction, and Col. J. N. Johnson, accompanied by Mr. Rice of the Courier, left for the purpose of going to Dent's Crossing and that vicinity, to treat with the Indians supposed to be friendly. They are then to make a detour and join the rest of the commission and escort at Graysonville.

I converged with two miners from the Mariposa region, just arrived, who informed me that an American was murdered between the Mariposa and Merced, a few days since, by Indians. They also report that a rumor was prevalent that another battle had occurred between the Indians and a company of rangers recently raised, but as they could tell nothing further it may be reasonably be set down as an idle rumor. Indian *stampedes* are now the order of the day.

Daily Alta California, June 17, 1851
Southern California

Ever since California changed her national allegiance, the southern section of it, especially the Los Angeles Valley, has endured all manner of oppressions from wild Indians and dissolute white men with far less conscience and much greater capacity and taste for evil than the untaught savage. The Mexican rule ceased, almost no law existed, and as did the Jews at a particular time in their history, "every man did that which seemed right in his own eyes." This might have been an almost enviable condition, had the inhabitants remained as before, free from the additions which the authority of the new flag allowed to quarter among them. There was not much danger of any very exciting scenes of disorder while the hospitable native California Dona possessed their ranches of princely acres, inhabited by the listless Indian, too superstitious and too indolent for enterprises of extenzive [*sic*] crime and daring.

Before the war some of the ranches occupied and cultivated by French and Americans, almost vied with the old Baronial estates of Europe in the number of their retainers as well as their wealth of flocks, herds and droves. But the results of the contest disorganized their households—for such might have been termed their Indian laborers—scattered them, and left the ranches uncultivated, and the stock exposed to the incursions of the Utah and other wild Indian tribes, and the no less unscrupulous inroads of professedly civilized men. The supremacy of the American arms imposed a new allegiance, but for a long time the ruling power afforded no protection in place of that which had existed previous to the war in the arms of the Indians and Californians, acting under the Mexican government.

Although a few soldiers stationed at the Cajon Pass would have almost entirely protected that whole section against the incursions of the marauding

Utahs and other Indian and white thieves who ate up in the mountains or sold at the Great Salt Lake, the horses and mules which they stole into the valleys below, from some cause or apathy on the part of the American military authority, the utmost that was effected was a visit in the Pass by General Smith and other officers, and a few troops for a while stationed at Ranch del Chino in the centre of the valley, out of all possible reach of preventing theft or punishing it. The rancheros have consequently been subjected to almost inevitable ruin. In a single night their horses and mules would be driven off and they left without even the means of pursuit.

Some eleven months ago, one of them for the fourteenth time within three years, had his cavalada swept away. Added to these forays are the oppressions from the lawless and reckless scum of our own countrymen and others, which the gold fever and new order of things generally had brought into the country. The city of Los Angeles became the headquarters of a gang, execrable beyond anything which we have experienced here. in the winter of 1849–50 a band of desperadoes put all law at defiance, and committed whatever crimes suited their depraved appetites with impunity. Over twenty men were killed there within four weeks. Since then the Morehead Expedition to the Colorado was in a great measure fitted out with mules and horses forcibly obtained and unpaid for. And finally bands of armed men roamed about the country, laying the different proprietors under such contributions as their needs, or caprice, or malignity dictated.

But at last the spirit was aroused, and, like our own citizens, the people of Los Angeles found it necessary to take effective measures. But the poor despised Indians had preceded them, and become the avengers of crime. The account of this transaction as given in the Los Angeles *Star*, and in our columns, will give the public a new idea of those Indians. Indolent and listless as the usually are, they are dangerous when aroused. That the party which they destroyed deserved their fate, there can be no doubt. That the atrocities which have turned on of the most beautiful sections of the continent into a Pandemonium, have been allowed so long to continue is disgraceful to the American name. It was the duty of the American government to protect the people, according to the stipulations of the treaty, as well in accordance with policy, justice, and humanity. Even the troops which might have been employed for this purpose were generally quartered near San Diego or at other places where there was no possible chance of their being of any service to anybody. It is to be hoped that the forces under Gen. Bean, the U.S. troops and the civil authorities will now act in concert and with energy, to put an end to the outrageous sets of the desperadoes who have ruled so long in that garden spot of California. The country is well worth the duty's performance, the people deserve it. A more hospitable class cannot be found of the continent than the native Californian of Spanish descent. That section of the state has been overshadowed by the golden dreams and realities of this, but its progress is no less sure and its future as promising, although its development has been and will be much more tardy.

Daily Alta California, February 14, 1851

INDIAN MURDERS.—Read the extract from the letter dated Los Angeles. it is strange, passing strange that the U.S. officer in command has never established a military post in the Cayon [sic] Pass. Two platoons of soldiers at that point could prevent the whole force of the Indians from passing and trepassing. It is through that pass that all the horses and mules stolen in the valley of Los Angeles are driven. A few soldiers there could effectually prevent all such traffic. We have again and again spoken of this subject. The people there deserve some protection by the United States forces.

Daily Alta California, February 18, 1853
Indian Disturbances in Mariposa

Lieut. Moore, arrived in town from Fort Miller, assures the *Republican* that nearly all the accounts relative to the Indian difficulties in that region have been grossly exaggerated. The particulars of the depredations of the Chowchillas were, in the main, correct; but the accounts of the killing of Mr. Converse and the attack on Fort Miller were mistakes altogether. The facts of the last case are: a mule was stolen from one of the camps, as was supposed, by the Indians. Lieut. Moore with a company followed the trail of the animal several miles, and finally reached the spot where it had been killed and part of it eaten. One or two arrows were still in the body of the mule, and they were recognized as the same used by the Merced Indians, a warlike and troublesome tribe.

In the Chowchilla difficulty the Indians say the whites fired first, while the whites as strenuously maintain that the Indians were the aggressors.

Daily Alta California, March 2, 1853
Train Attacked by Indians

The *Union* has a correspondence from Shasta, dated 20th February, giving an account of an attack on a provision train by the Indians near Yreka:

"Intelligence was to-day received of the murder on Friday last, of one man Dick Owen, and the entire loss of the pack train Mr. Archer, of thirteen mules and one horse, and also the cargoes upon the animals. The train was on the way up to Yreka, and was crossing the Sugar Loaf Mountains, forty miles above here, when they suddenly found themselves surrounded by a large body of Indians who made an attack upon the train then traveling—Mr. Archer losing his entire train everything he had with him, being compelled to leave the body of Mr. Owen on the trail. Mr. N. Horsley whose train was in the immediate neighborhood at the time, had a number of his mules wounded, but succeeded in making his escape, it is believed without any further damage. Mr. H was also on his way to Yreka. There are trains which have been some days overdue from Yreka, and their non-appearance creates much anxiety."

Daily Alta California, March 4, 1853

A report is in town that the Indians have fired the steam saw mill of the Tuolumne County Water Company. Of the truth of it I cannot speak as 'tis but a rumor. 'Tis known that the Indians in that section are very hostile and inclined to mischief. If this report prove true they may look out for a good drubbing.

P.P.

Daily Alta California, March 6, 1853
SACRAMENTO NEWS
[PER ADAM'S & CO.'S EXPRESS]
Exciting News from Tehama-Indian Thefts-Terrible Vengeance of the Whites

Mr. Lurk of Adams & Co., furnished the *Union* with the following exciting news.

The Indians have committed so many depredations in the North, of late, that the people are enraged against them, and are ready to knife them, shoot them, or inoculate them with small pox—all of which have been done.

Some time since, the Indians in Colusa county destroyed about some $5,000 worth of stock belonging to Messrs. Thomas & Toombe; since which time they have had two men employed, at $8.00 per month' to hunt down and kill the Diggers, like other beasts of prey. On Friday, the 25th ult., one of these men, named John Breckenridge, was alone, and armed only with a bowie knife, when he met with four Indians and attacked them. They told him to leave, and commenced shooting arrows at him; but, undaunted, he continued to advance, and succeeded in killing one, and taking one prisoner, while the other two escaped. He immediately proceeded to Moon's Ranch, where the captured Indian was hung by the citizens.

On Friday, the 25th Feb., stock was stolen from Mr. Carter of Butte county, to the value of $3,000. Mr. Carter went forthwith to the camp of the well known stage proprietors, Messrs. Hall & Crandall, and the men started with a party of twelve men in search of the Indian depredators. After a fruitless search in the vicinity of Pine and Deer Creeks, the party became impatient and dispersed in Sunday evening and returned home, one detachment of the party discovered a half-breed by the name of Battedou, and took him prisoner. The man, fearing for his own life, agreed to show the cave where the Indians were concealed, if they would release him. Notice was sent round and the people assembled again at Oak Grove on Monday, from which they started at midnight for the cave.

Arriving there at early daylight on Tuesday morning, rocks were rolled into the cave, and the wretched inmates, rushing out for safety, met danger a thousand times more dreadful. The first one that made his appearance was shot by Capt. Geo Rose, and the others met the same fate from the rifles of the Americans. Altogether, there were thirteen killed; three chiefs of different rancherias, and three women. Three women and five children were spared; and it is but doing justice to say, that the women who were killed were placed in front as a sort of breast-work and killed either by accident or mistake. Capt. Rose took one child, Mr. Lattimer another, and the others were disposed of in the same charitable manner among the party.

On Tuesday night, March 1st, three work oxen belonging to Messrs. Bull and Baker were stolen from a corral in Shasta city, and on Thursday morning twenty-six head were driven off Red Bluffs; value near $4,000.

Daily Alta California, March 31, 1853

The Los Angeles *Star* from the 1st to the 26th came to hand.

A delegation of thirty-two Cahuila [Cahuilla] Indians paid a visit to Mr. Wilson, Indian Agent at Los Angles, to whom they made the following complaint:

"That Mr. Weaver, at San Gorgonio, has annoyed them by shooting their animals, and imposing upon them in various ways for some time past; and that to their repeated protestations, he pays no regard. Mr. Wilson was unable to afford them any redress or relief, as their case comes within the civil jurisdiction of the state, but he has requested the justice of the peace at San Bernardino to take the matter in hand and look into the facts."

The *Star* says, "we have been blessed with an abundance of rain during the past week, and the vegetation of all kinds is now in a forward state.

A man by the name of Woods of Louisiana was attacked by a bear on the 22nd ult. while on a trading expedition among the Indians, and after a severe and hard-fought battle, succeeded in killing it; not, however, without sustaining severe wounds upon his person from the effects of which he died about seven days after.

The great horse-race between Fashion and Greasy Puss came off at Los Angeles without satisfactory results. One of the mares threw her rider and bolted the track. The judge decided that it was no race, and proposed another trial.

Each Sunday morning, says the *Star*, our streets are filled with drunken Indians, male and female. It is within bounds to set down the number of filthy drooling beasts, in human shape, at one hundred. Who knows how or where they procure the rotgut stuff that makes them thus. One thing, however, is known, namely; that they are beastly drunk, and further, that there is a heavy fine for vending liquor to them; but we do not know, with these hundred abominations staring our whole community in the face, in broad daylight, every Sunday, that efforts are made to discover who has done it.

On the night of the 15th last, another Indian foray was made to the neighborhood of Santa Ana. The extent of the depredation is not fully ascertained, but thus far it is known that eight horses that were picketed down were stolen, one killed and another badly wounded with arrows. To what extent these evils are to be continued, it is difficult to surmise. But little doubt is entertained that other forays will yet be made, from the fact that Indians supposed to be Pah [Paiute, perhaps Chemehuevi] have within a few days past been observed sulking in the mountains. Col. Williams has lost 75 gentle horses and mules with others belonging to persons residing in the Pueblo and the vicinity. The band was trailed to Cahon Pass [Cajon], but there all traces ceased, owing to the heavy rains which intervened, and there the matter rests.

The Indians in Los Angeles county are becoming so troublesome to the rancheros that a public meeting is proposed for the purpose of devising a plan for the protection of property.

Daily Alta California, April 12, 1853
Fight with the Indians at Yreka
YREKA, April 3, 1853

I hasten to inform you of our safe arrival at this place a few days ago. We, Goldsmith and myself, had to encounter many hardships and difficulties before reaching our destination, at one time being compelled to fight. The Indians were about attacking our train, which was rather large, comprising

over 70 mules. After half an hour's struggle, we succeeded in getting the better of them, but not without wounds. Two of our Spaniards were slightly, and
another one was, as we then supposed, mortally wounded; we, however,
brought him to Yreka, where he is likely to recover. We lost not one of our
mules.

Daily Alta California, June 12, 1853

INDIAN TROUBLES.-The Indians about Sonora are said to be exceedingly troublesome. Complaints are made that they are in the habit of stealing the animals of farmers and running them off into the defiles of the mountains. A
short time since they stole a span of splendid horses, valued at $500, which,
despite immediate pursuit made by a party of Americans, they succeeded in
carrying off. They are said to number about six hundred men. One of the sufferers is anxious to raise a force of sixty men and chastise them.

San Francisco Bulletin, January 21, 1860

The Indians have again become very troublesome to the settlers of
Mendocino county. Mr. White, a resident of Long Valley, informs us that they
have become so bad that the settlers have been compelled to organize themselves into a standing army, so to speak, and by taking turns keep their stock
and homes under constant guard. For some time previous to this being done,
the gentleman alone, Mr. Woodman, had lost 109 head of horses, 74 of which
were found dead in a canon not far from his place, and upon the bodies of
which the Indians were having a good feast. On the 19th of December, the
settlers turned out, and attacking the enemy succeeded in killing 32 and taking two prisoners. The United States troops located in that region are represented to be pursuing, during all these troubles, a "masterly course of
inactivity." The aid of the State has therefore been asked, and will we trust be
granted. (As quoted in *They Were Only Diggers*, p. 42.)

Sutter's Fort in present-day Sacramento with an American Indian entering at the far right. From Revere, *A Tour of Duty in California,* 1849.

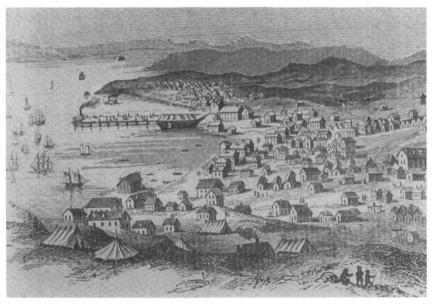

San Francisco during the Gold Rush. From Buck, *A Yankee Trader in the Gold Rush,* 1930.

Thousands of miners arrived in California through San Francisco in 1849. Note the number of ships in San Francisco Bay. From Taylor, *California Life*, 1858.

Sutter's Mill at the village of Koloma. From Taylor, *California Life*, 1858.

Sacramento's J Street as it appeared in 1853, a trading center for the Northern Mines. From Buck, *A Yankee Trader in the Gold Rush*, 1930.

Sacramento, 1849. From Letts, *California Illustrated*, 1852.

Sacramento during the flood of 1852. From Taylor, *Eldorado*, 1859.

Yreka, California, not far from the Oregon border, became a mining town in the heart of Indian country. From Buck, *A Yankee Trader in the Gold Rush*, 1930.

Nested in the shadow of Mount Shasta was the mining town of Shasta, 1854. From Grabhorn, *A California Gold Rush Miscelleny*, 1934.

Miners washing sand and gravel with a Long Tom. From *Harper's New Monthly Magazine*, volume 20.

California Indian miners punishing fellow miner. From Gerstacker, *Gerstackers' Travels*, 1854.

California Indians moved from ranches with their families to work in the mines from 1848 to 1850. From Forbes, *California*, 1937.

California Indians often interacted with non-natives in a peaceful manner as seen here. From Revere, *A Tour of Duty in California,* 1849.

Traditional lives of California Indians were transformed by the Gold Rush. From Bartlett, *Personal Narrative of Explorations,* 1854.

California Indian miners working the placers. From *Hutchings' Illustrated California Magazine*, 1859.

California Indian miners. From Bartlett, *Personal Narratives of Exploration*, 1854.

California Indian woman washing gold with a pan. From Hutchings' *Illustrated California Magazine*, 1859.

An attack of a California Indian village. From Browne, *Harper's New Monthly Magazine*, 1861.

★★

Chapter 3

OTHER NATIVE RESISTANCE

Truly, raiding white Americans during the Gold Rush was a significant and successful form of resistance. Yet the indigenous inhabitants of California did not limit their protest to this one strategy. Native Americans employed other methods to express their opposition to the non-Indian invasion of California. For instance, as a couple of documents demonstrate, Indians frequently directed their efforts at Chinese miners, demanding money and goods.

Other newspaper articles in this section suggest a multitude of tactics. Besides stealing from Anglos and Chinese, Indians defended their homelands by attacking American settlements, burning ranches, and killing whites. They ambushed mail carriers, merchants, miners, and anyone else who trespassed on their lands. Native Americans working on ranches often left their jobs to join other indigenous peoples in coordinated strikes against whites. According to one report, Indians surprised and killed seventy-two Anglos near a small stream known as Rattlesnake Creek. Some fought American militia units, thereby dispelling earlier rumors among California's Anglo population that the region's native people never engaged in combat.

After the establishment of Indian reservations in the Golden State, Anglos sought to capture Native Americans and place them on these reserves. Indians manifested their disdain for this oppressive system by bolting the reservations at every possible opportunity. Anglos, in response, searched for Native Americans who left the reserves. Whites occasionally provided food and clothing to Indians in exchange for promises that they would cease stealing livestock belonging to American citizens. As one document implies, Indians in at least one instance defiantly broke their promises by stealing some items from their captors' camp and escaping into safer regions.

71

One newspaper article reveals that even Indian youth refused to kowtow to Anglo demands. A Native American boy, perhaps only ten or twelve years old, attempted to burn down the house of one Colonel Stevenson. Although he apparently did not succeed in completely destroying the home, he nonetheless publicly exhibited his aversion to the increasing presence of foreigners within his native land. Resistance knew no age limits.

Daily Alta California, January 13, 1851

ANOTHER INDIAN SKIRMISH.—On Friday last, some fifty Indians attacked a small party of men, some half dozen in number, while they were at work in the vicinity of Pleasant Valley, in locating a ranch. They were about five miles north-east of Johnson's ranch, in El Dorado county.

We understand that the attack was made when the whites were not expecting any thing of the kind, but Major Wm. Graham had spent too much of his time in the Rocky Mountains to be totally unprepared and quick as the nature of the case would admit, his men were armed, and fought the Indians according to their own mode of warfare, from behind trees and rocks. The result of the fight was nine Indians killed and one white man wounded in the leg by a rifle ball.

It is the intention of Maj. Graham to locate a ranch in Pleasant Valley, which will be the furthest outpost on our eastern frontier, and not far distant from the immigrant road.—*Sacramento Transcript.*

Daily Alta California, January 14, 1851

FURTHER INDIAN TROUBLES.—It will be seen by reference to the letter of our correspondent at San Jose, that an express arrived on Sunday from the Mariposa region, representing that there had been further outrages committed by the Indians, and calling upon the Executive for men and arms to protect them from the incursions of their wild neighbors.

Daily Alta California, January 20, 1851

INDIAN TROUBLES.—There was a rumor in town yesterday, that a severe fight had taken place between the Indians and whites, in the vicinity of Burns', in which fifty Indians were killed and wounded, and fiften [sic] whites.

Another rumor was that a party of Indians made a descent upon a camp on the San Joaquin, killing and wounding all its inmates, some half a dozen in number; and sending a message to Savage, by one of the plains in the vicinity of the San Joaquin, they would give him and his party a fair fight.— *Stockton paper.*

Daily Alta California, January 21, 1851
Indian Difficulties

By reference to the letter of our special correspondent at the Capital, it will be seen that there is additional intelligence of Indian disturbances. An express was received on Sunday evening from Mariposa county, announcing the fact that a battle had been fought between the whites and Indians of Mariposa county. The Indians were entrenched at one of their villages, but were driven off with a loss of about sixty killed and from ten to twenty wounded. It also appears that *seventy-two* Americans were surprised and murdered by the Indians, near Rattlesnake creek. Prompt and efficient measures will soon be necessary to quiet the Indians, and we doubt if in the present state of affairs, it will be possible to treat with them without recourse to arms. Our Indian commissioners must bestir themselves if they expect to be of service to the people of California. For information as to the course contemplated by our State authorities, we refer our readers to the letter of our correspondent.

Daily Alta California, February 4, 1851

But toe [*sic*] most important intelligence we are in recept [*sic*] of is that the Pitt River Indians in that vicinity are exceedingly troublesome. Our informant started for Scott's River with a small party, and while in camp one night had his mules all driven off by the Indians. The party started in pursuit and were routed. Falling back, they were reinforoed [*sic*], and went out again, numbering eighty men.

The Indians fought them desperately among the hills, and not only routed them but drove them completely out of that section of the country. Two days afterward the Indians attacked a train of pack mules, and having cut the train in two, succeeded in capturing half in advance.

Daily Alta California, February 5, 1851

PITT'S RIVER INDIANS.—The *Transcript* gives an account of two fights between those Indians and emigrants to Scott's river in both of which the whites were completely routed and driven out of that section of the country.

Daily Alta California, February 7, 1851

INDIAN FIGHT.—See Mr. Wilson's letter, giving an account of Savage's second fight with the Indians. We have received from another reliable source an account of the same affair, differing but little from the one we publish. Our correspondence says in addition, "that most of the warriors from the rancheros are unaccountably absent, and the belief is that they are with the hostile Indians."

Daily Alta California, February 14, 1851
LOS ANGELES, Feb. 4, 1851.

News has reached us that the Tulare Indians have killed Danton's party and Capt. Dorsey's party. Don Henrique himself was here at the time, after more horses and provisions, as his horses had failed, and he was under the necessity of making a *coral* [corral] at the Four Creeks. There seems no doubt of his *vaqueros* together with Capt. Dorsey and his party, who coralled with Dalton, or near by, having all been killed and the cattle dispersed. French's ranch was attacked by the same Indians, who appear to have been several hundred strong, armed with bows and arrows. Fortunately an emigrating party of 40 Americans were at the ranch at the time. The Indians were repulsed with the loss of about forty killed. A dispatch reached us the past week from French, asking arms and cartridges; they were immediately forwarded by one of his partners, who was in the city at the time. Why cannot a [military] post be established there? It is highly important for the trade of this valley and Stockton, Sacramento and San Francisco. Thirteen men in all are reported to have been massacred at the Four Creeks. Capt. Dorsey is from San José. You can rely upon this news, as it comes to us in veritable form. Don Henrique is now on his return to the Four Creeks, with a party of about a dozen men, hoping to form a connection with the emigrants who are at French's.

The election for Senator in the place of Hope will take place on the 17th inst. (next Monday.) You may expect Mr. Hope's successor in San José about the last of this month. No candidates are yet announced, neither can I divine who will be elected.

Yours, very respectfully, LEWIS GRANGER

THE INDIAN EXPEDITION—Col. McKee and the escort of Indian Commissioners left Stockton on Wednesday morning last.

Daily Alta California, February 4, 1853
SAN JOAQUIN NEWS
Indian Difficulties—Fight on the Chowchilla

A slip from the Stockton *Journal,* by Todd's express, has a letter from Mariposa, giving the details of a fight between the Indians and some miners.

MARIPOSA, Jan 31.

It appears that parties living on the lower Mariposa, and on the Chowchilla, have lost, during the winter, a considerable number of horses, and mules, without being able to discover the marauders.

At last a large fine horse was stolen, and being well shod, his larger deep footprints in the soft earth led the party in search of him to the rancherias of about one hundred Indians, men, women and children, situated near the Chowchilla.

The Americans, five or six in number, before approaching the village, dismounted and hitched their horses, and advanced on foot. The Indians seemed indisposed to parley, *no sabe, no sabe,* being their only reply to the questions propounded to them.

One of the party by the name Starkie, perceiving some beligerent [*sic*] movements on the part of the savages, fired his rifle killing their leader, and fell himself almost at the same instant pierced with several arrows. The fight then became general.

Dr. Westfall was severely wounded in his pistol hand and, discovering that the Indians were about to cut them off from their horses, they retreated, leaving Starkie on the ground. A day or two after this event, another party returned.

And the Indians, who had taken alarm at their approach, had fled from their village. The party burned the village, with all their provisions, traps, &c., and retired.

Daily Alta California, February 5, 1853

INDIAN NEWS—In addition to the news contained in the communications in another column, we hear a report that the Indians have attacked Fort Miller, and also killed Mr. Converse at Converse's Ferry, on the San Joaquin, and carried out his wife into captivity. Four hunters, who formerly made regular visits into Mariposa, from the Chowchilla, are also reported as missing. These are only straggling rumors.

Daily Alta California, February 10, 1853
SACRAMENTO NEWS
ADAMS & CO.'S EXPRESS

DRY CREEK INDIANS.—The Indians on Dry Creek have succeeded in escaping from their fortified position, and are supposed to have taken shelter in the *tules.* The war of extermination has thus been for the present, suspended.

Daily Alta California, March 18, 1853
Shasta Mining Matters

The *Courier* of Saturday, says that during the past two months, the Indians throughout the northern portions of California have been untiring in acts of hostility against the whites.

Daily Alta California, May 5, 1853

On the night of Tuesday, 26 ult., Capt. McDermitt and several companions had four mules shot with arrows, about seven miles above French Gulch. Messrs. P. and H. saw some fifteen or twenty Indians at the same place on Thursday, and accelerated their motion down the mountain by a few doses of Colt's pills.

Sacramento Union, June 6, 1853

A writer from Sonora to the *Republican* gives the following ludicrous anecdote:

It is reported that a party of six "digger" Indians came down from the mountains of a few days since and when near Jesse Brush's residence, on the Tuolumne, they met an equal number of Chinamen. The chief advanced and demanded their poll-tax. This they obstinately refused to pay. The chief then demanded of them to show their receipts. They refused to do this also. The Indian then shot one of them, whereupon they capitulated and paid over $18. The "diggers" then returned, evidently well satisfied.

San Francisco Bulletin, May 31, 1859

A few days ago, the Indian boy who set fire to the house of Col. Stevenson, was taken from the custody of Sheriff Dunn, by a number of citizens, and hanged. The Sheriff had taken him to the Court House and left him in a room adjoining the Court room, and while absent for a few moments, the boy was taken by the mob. This is really horrible, and reflects no credit to the parties concerned. The Beacon condemns the act in a very severe manner, by alluding to it in "eloquent silence." The boy was but twelve or fifteen years of age. (The Tehama Gazette says that he was only ten years old) What good will the hanging of this stripling accomplish? Will it deter other Indian boys from committing a similar act? If so, the act is defensible. If not, appreciating the magnitude of his crime, is very true; but why not let him be hung in a legal manner? There was no danger of his escaping.

San Francisco Bulletin, November 14, 1859
Soldier killed by Squaw

A party of four soldiers recently abused a squaw at Hoopa, and the squaw resisted stabbing one of the party fatally. An investigation was to take place.

San Francisco Bulletin, January 14, 1860

In the *Sonora Democrat* a correspondent, writing from Long Valley, Mendocino County, of date 20th December, gives some Capt. Jarboe's campaign against them. He says: . . . The Eel River Rangers, under the command of Capt. Jarboe, have been doing the most valuable and effective service in quelling the Indians. A portion of his command (13 men) were here several days lately, and were active in assisting us in pursuing and chastising the guilty parties. . . . The command, while going from this to Jarboe's headquarters, had a pitched battle with some 90 Indians on South Eel River, and I think it was the most desperate fight I have known with the Indians in California. . . . About 30 were slain, and as many more wounded, of as thieving, marauding Indians as ever roamed the forests of California. This refutes the statement of Major Johnson, U.S.A., who has said the Indians would never fight.

This company of rangers has been compelled to kill a great number of Indians. Women and children are in all cases taken prisoners when practicable, and well fed and protected during their stay in camp, and while being removed to the reservations.

A member of Capt. Jarboe's party, has just arrived here, who says that the company had a severe fight near Round Valley, on the 13th inst., and killed some 30 bucks, and took 28 prisoners.

San Francisco Bulletin, January 14, 1860

Capt. S. D. Goodrich sends to the Napa Reporter a letter to him from Capt.
Jarboe (now engaged in a campaign against the Indians of the Eel River country, Humboldt county), dated Fort Defiance, 28th November, from which the
following extracts are taken:

I had considerable trouble in getting the prisoners to the Mendocino
Reservation, that I started with on the 25th October. I succeeded, however, in
getting 90 there, 10 bucks took leg bail across the mountains, and are now at
large, engaged in killing stock. I have had 4 engagements with the Indians
since your party left here—26th of October. On the 18th inst. was the last, in
which one of my men was wounded and 7 Indians killed. The Indians had 2
cattle and one hog in camp. notwithstanding I whip them in every fight,
make many presents to the prisoners, and hold out great inducements to
bring them to peace, they continue committing depredations. I have had 6
old Indians here for 2 weeks, gave them plenty to eat, good clothing, and
promised them to do the same by all their tribe, provided they would not kill
any more stock belonging to the whites. Last night, during a rain storm, they
stole some things, and left for parts unknown.

San Francisco Bulletin, March 2, 1861

The steamer Columbia arrived here last night about half-past 6 o'clock from
ports on the Northern coast, bringing papers from Humboldt Bay to the 23rd
February, and from Crescent City to the 16th.

The Humboldt Times is filled with notices of "outrages" by the Indians on
the settlers, and the killing of large numbers of the former by the white men.
That journal of the 9th February, has the following items on the subject:

About a week ago, thirty-nine diggers were killed by some settlers, on
main Eel river, above the crossing of the old Sonoma trail. It seems that a few
settlers at Ketinshou, at the beginning of winter, in order to avoid danger to
their stock from snow, moved down on main Eel river, at the point mentioned. not long since some of them returned to look after their houses, etc.,
and found that the Indians had destroyed all that they had left. Hereupon a
party started in pursuit of the offenders, taking along some friendly Indians
to assist them. They report having found the band that committed the damage and killed the above number of bucks.

The settlers of Upper Mattole on Saturday last made an attack on a band
of predatory Indians (in fact, all the Digger tribe would come under that
head,) and killed seven of their number. The Indians had previously, as usual,

made it a practice to run off and kill stock, but not being satisfied with that, had made an attempt the day before to take the life of one of the settlers—an elderly gentleman whose name we could not learn. They shot at him with arrows, one of which struck him, but not so as to inflict a serious wound.

The same journal of date 23rd February says: A band of Indians killed and drove off several head of cattle and a lot of hogs from settlers on Kneeland's Prairie last week, whereupon a party of men went in pursuit of the rascals, came up in the redwoods near North Yager Creek, and killed four of their number.

Ketinshou Valley was sacked by the Indians on Friday last, by watching the only settler there, John Fulwider, until he went for his cow in the evening , and then rushed into the house. They shot the dog and fired at Fulwider on his return. Having nothing to defend himself with he had to leave. He went over to Eel River, to the settlement, which was abandoned on Sunday last, for the reason that there was too many Indians about. They had killed about 300 of their hogs and a great number of stock On their way in they came across the Indians that had robbed Larabee's house, and killed two of them. They went on to the house, or to where it had stood, and found that the Indians had burned it and killed Ann Quinn—cook at the ranch. They found the body of Ann lying about six feet from the door considerably burnt. David King was plowing a short distance from the house at the time and when he heard the firing, started towards it. The Indians saw him coming and fired at him, attempted to cut off his retreat, but he succeeded in effecting his escape. The names of the men that came down are G. Abbott, J. Bartlett, A. Posey, John Dewey, S. Fleming, and Pierce Asbill. They arrived at Larabee's place, which is on Van Duzen Fork, about three hours after the house was attacked. The men recovered about three horse loads of the plunder.

We have not received a mail from the south for two weeks, and it is the general conviction that the mail rider has been intercepted and killed by the Indians between Long Valley and Hydesville.

Marysville Appeal, July 30, 1865

Last Saturday, eight Indians visited Fairfield Bar, on Middle Feather river, as Chinese Tax Collectors. Two old Chinamen were politely requested to pungle down their "Poll Tax," when they presented their receipts. The "lords of the forest" assured the Johns that said paper was "no good," nothing short of cash would satisfy the demand. The Johns having no money, the tax collectors knocked them down and appropriated all the rice, pork, and other valuables in their cabin. (As quoted in *The Destruction of California Indians*, p. 290.)

Chapter 4

★★

THE GOLD RUSH AND NATIVE AMERICANS
OF SOUTHERN CALIFORNIA

The Gold Rush certainly brought about a significant amount of change in the lives of Native Americans living in or near the mines. Yet the invasion of non-Indians into California directly affected indigenous peoples throughout the entire region. Soon, thousands of Anglos converged on Southern California, upsetting the traditional lifestyles of the Chumash, Quechans, Luisenos, Kumeyaay, Chemehuevos, Cupenos, Cahuillas, Gabrilenos, Juanenos, and others. Whites suddenly—and sometimes gradually—seized the prized homelands of these peoples because they assumed that Indians had no right to retain such extensive property.

Native Americans responded to this incursion in various ways. For instance, Antonio Garra and the Cupenos sought to ally with other native societies and expel the American invaders from the area. However, Garra's approach conflicted sharply with the views of Juan Antonio and the Cahuillas, who generally and pragmatically befriended the whites of Southern California. Ironically, Juan Antonio and the Cahuillas captured Antonio Garra, thus ending Garra's plan for a major pan-Indian uprising in 1851.

The following documents focus on the Garra Revolt as well as on relations between the Cahuillas and whites. Some newspaper articles particularly reflect the panic and excitement that abounded during Garra's attempt to organize a large-scale assault against Anglos and Californians. Americans in northern California avidly read these reports. This information only confirmed their prejudices regarding the indigenous peoples of Calfiornia and likely exacerbated tensions in the gold fields. A few articles discuss the alliance between the Cahuillas and the Lugo family of San Bernadino, which resulted in a violent encounter between Juan Antonio's men and American thieves in May 1851. Subsequent documents relate the tenuous relations that prevailed between local Americans and the Cahuillas over the next few months.

Los Angeles Star, May 31, 1851
Terrible Tragedy

"About two months since, a party of men, some 25 in number, arrived at the place and encamped a short distance from the city. They were under the command of Capt. John Irving said to be an old Texas ranger. We do not suppose that many persons here were informed as to the objects of the company. Irving gave out that he was going to Sonora to fight the Indians. One member of the company, in endeavoring to induce a citizen to join them, stated that they were going to Mexico to rob some of the specie conductas between the mines and Mazatlan. When here, they excited the terror of the citizens, and many offences [sic] were charged upon them. About ten days since they took their departure, moving in the direction of the Colorado, and probably not one in ten of our citizens supposed they should ever again hear of the party.

"On Sunday last, letters were received in town from Col. Magruder, at Chino, and Mayor Wilson, representing a state of things which seemed to indicate that actual war existed between Irving's men and the native Californians. It was said that Irving and his party were killing cattle, stealing horses, and conducting themselves in such a lawless manner as to render it necessary that they should be speedily checked.

"In the course of the forenoon a public meeting was held in the court house. Addresses were made by various citizens, and suggestions made as to a proper course of action. The prevailing opinion seemed to be that it was advisable that the men should be pursued and brought to justice. There was much excitment in the community and all our citizens were prompt in denouncing the marauders.

"The Sheriff summoned a posse, and on Monday morning proceeding to Chino where it was represented that forces were concentrating—The Sherriff was armed with a warrant, issued by Jonathon R. Scott, Esq., for the arrest of Irving's party on the charge of grand larceny.

"On Tuesday morning the Sheriff proceed to Rubidoux's ranch, where they were informed that Irving had encamped. There on the previous night, Rubidoux says that they treated him very civilly, and up to the time the Sheriff could obtain no authentic information of any serious depredations having been committed. From spies sent to Temescal, it was ascertained that a body of men, supposed to be Irving's men, had crossed over toward Lugo's on Tuesday morning, and the Sherriff, fearing they had gone there for no good purpose, deemed it advisable to follow them.

"The Sheriff had not proceeded far before he learned that Irving's party had been killed by the Apolitans, a tribe of Cowie Indians. The story seemed at first to be improbable, and gained but little credence. As they proceeded, however, it gathered confirmation, and at last was made certain by eye-witnesses. From various sources we have collected information concerning this tragic affair. The full particulars of every thing connected with the transaction, will probably never be ascertained, at least not until a judicial investigation has been held, and great caution is needed to guard against exaggerated statements. In the following account, we have aimed to give only such facts as are corroborated by men of veracity.

"It appears that Irving's party first went to Filipe Lugo's and broke and entered the house. Whether or not they stole any thing of value, is not certain. They ransacked the trunks and scattered the clothing about, and probably took away some articles of small value. Then they proceeded to Jose Maria Lugo's some six miles distant from Felipe's. The people at the ranches fled at their approach, but it does not appear that they entered any houses except those of the Lugos. At Jose Maria Lugo's it is said that they stole various articles. It is the prevailing opinion that the object was to murder the two young Lugos. Various circumstance tend to strengthen this belief. Their animosity towards the Lugos was very strong, and if they had fallen in with them, undoubtedly would have assassinated them.

"Irving had been heard to say that he would take the scalps of the young Lugos, and there can be little doubt that he was bent on murder as well as plunder.

"Not finding the Lugos at home, Irving left the premises, and struck into a road leading to the mountains. He must have supposed that he could gain the valley beyond, or he would never allowed himself to be surrounded in the manner which he was.

"The Cowies, many of whom are domicillated at Lugos, followed up Irving's party, and attacked them with bows and arrows and lances. Irving followed the road into a ravine, the steep banks of which prevented his egress, and here it was that the whole party was slain. Not one was left to tell the tale. The Indians first shot them down with arrows and then beat in their skulls with stones. Persons who have seen the dead bodies describe them as being mangled in a manner shocking to behold.

"Those who are known to be killed are John Irving, Frank Wilson, Perely, Jack Hitchcock, Charles Lavelle, and George Clarke. Besides these men, there were known to be _____, when he left here, Wm. O'Donnell, Peter (supposed to be the brother of O'Donnell) A Spencer, Ma___, Bogel and three men Mac, Sam and Pat. It is possible that the three last named are included among the fore group, who [whose] Christian names are not given.

Only one Indian was killed and two or three wounded, so far as can be ascertained. Some supposed that a larger number were killed, and that the Indians conceal their actual loss. We are inclined to believe that but one was killed. The Indian known to have been killed was an alcalde of the Apolitans, and was cut off from the main body and shot, as is said, by Irving.

The Indians were headed by Ricardo, a native Californian, and one who has been in many affrays.

"The force of the Indians is variously stated. The most reliable accounts represent that they had from 300 to 400 men in the conflict. A portion of them were mounted.

"The Indians say that Irving, or the man who appeared to be the captain of the party, fought very bravely. He was mounted on a superb horse and was conspicuous throughout the engagement, encouraging his men, and charging into the very midst of his opponents. He was found with five arrow wounds in the region of the heart.

"It is supposed that Irving's men had about $5,000 with them, all of which fell into the hands of the Indians. They exhibit their booty freely to all who visit the rancheria.

"The bodies were found entirely naked, the Indians having stripped them of their clothes, which, together with the arms and horses they carried off to the rancheria, as spoils of war.

"It does indeed appear almost incredible that twelve well-armed men, most of whom had seen service in Texas, and all of whom fought desperately, should have been conquered by Indians and all slain, while their antagonists sustained a loss of but one of their number. But it must be remembered that they fought at a great disadvantage. So long as they kept upon the plain, they could offer a resistance to their pursuers, with some show of success. But the moment they entered the canada their doom was sealed. The Indians easily gained access to the hills above, and if Irving's party had consisted of twice or even thrice of twelve men, they must all have fallen an easy prey. Those who have viewed the scene of conflict are not at all surprised at the result.

"It seems probable that the Indians were impressed with the idea that they had authority to pursue these men. Years ago the authorities here gave to the chief of the Apolitans mission a direction to capture all thieves who might infest their neighborhood, and it is stated that more recently this authority has been renewed by the Judge of one of our courts." (As quoted in *Scrapbook of Benjamin Hayes*, Volume 38, Bancroft Library, University of California, Berkeley.)

Los Angeles Star, May 31, 1851

"Nothing has been talked about during the past week except the fate of John Irving and his men. Business had been checked, and men gather in small knots and discuss the probability of the affair. We fear that no new facts will be elicited at the coroner's inquest and that the circumstances attending this tragedy will never be fully known. Irving and his party were well known in the community, as they were in town nearly two months prior to their final departure." (As quoted in *Scrapbook of Benjamin Hayes*, Volume 38, Bancroft Library, University of California, Berkeley.)

Los Angeles Star, June 7, 1851
Coroner's Inquest
Part of testimony of Stephen C. Foster:

After the battle, Foster along with other posse members entered the ravine where he "saw the bodies of ten Americans; they were naked, and the men appeared to have been killed with arrows and their heads beaten with stones; the bodies had from five to nine arrow wounds, except that appeared to have been killed by beating upon the head with stones. The bodies were unmutilated, and, the features fresh and easily distinguished. I was informed that more bodies were up high on a hill that hung over the ravine and I saw a number of buzzards flying around, but I did not go up to see the bodies. The eyes of one man, said to be Capt. Irving, had been picked out by buzzards."

Part of testimony of Jesus Castro:

When the Indians overtook the Americans, neither party spoke to each other. The Indians yell in their usual mode. We were near enough to speak to them and the fight continued thus the whole way. In fighting, the Americans would stop and fire numerous shots, and then push on. The Indians would sometimes dismount from their horses, run on, shoot arrow, and again mount their horses. The parties never came nearer than a hundred yards, and the arrows did not reach the Americans. (As quoted in *Scrapbook of Benjamin Hayes*, Volume 38, Bancroft Library, University of California, Berkeley.)

Los Angeles Star, November 20, 1851
Interview with George Evans:

Evans survived the massacre in San Timoteo Canyon and returned to Los Angeles in the fall of 1851 where he gave the following interview.

The gang had been at the home of Jose Maria Lugo for only a few minutes, "when they saw a large body of Indians advancing towards the house from the direction of Apolitan. They immediately mounted, and resumed the road. As the Indians approached, a hasty council was held, when Irving insisted on retreating, to which Evans strongly objected urging him to fight the Indians at once, as the only means of securing a successful passage along their road, which led through the mountains, to that taken by their companions who had been sent ahead. Irving's will prevailed, and this, according to Evans was the cause of the catastrophe. They occasionally fired at the Indians as they came near, but in the main kept up a rapid retreat until they reached the forks in the road, where Evans again begged Irving to fight, but in vain. He also advised him to keep the road, but Irving, as if doomed, turned into the mountains, along the path which led into the fatal trip where they were caught and killed. It was here that Evans, seeing that they were lost, determined upon attempting to escape. He was here, as generally, riding in the rear of the men, who were making all speed for the hills. When near the chapparel [sic], his horse stopped and refused to go further.— Seizing his pistols from his holsters, Evans pushed on afoot, the savages almost at his heels. The chapparel [sic] is thick along the path and a limb knocked off his hat. Just there the road made a sudden turn, and he dashed in a clump of bushes, which offered the only hope of eluding pursuit. Almost instantly the Indians passed, one of them stopping to pick up Evan's hat. Soon Evans heard a few shots, followed by moments of dreadful silence, and then a few shots more. Thus he lay still near dark, when a cart passed, which he supposed contained the dead and wounded Indians, as much crying or lamentation accompanied it. From time to time, various parties passed returning. At length, a Californian, mounted on a fine horse, rode right up to his hiding place, seeming to be in search of him. Evan waited to catch his eye, intending then to shoot, and, if possible, seize the horse and escape. It was a moment of terrible suspense, eluded by another Californian on the hill-side telling his companion to 'come on.' The other immediately left. Evans remained in the hiding place until dark, when all returning parties seemed to have passed. The strangest part of his adventure remains to be told, and we have no reason to doubt its truth. Evans followed the Indians directly back to the house of Jose Maria Lugo, (about eighty miles); there he found a mule saddled which he took and fled towards Temascal [sic], subsequently joining the company of Sonorenian miners near the Colorado, telling them that Irving would be on shortly. The true state of the case did not leak out until they had crossed the river, when, as if only then relieved from his terror, Evans exclaimed, 'Thank God I am safe!' (As quoted in

Scrapbook of Benjamin Hayes, Volume 38, Bancroft Library, University of California, Berkeley.)

Los Angeles Star, June 14, 1851

We give a translation of the arrangement made by the County Judge and others with Juan Antonio, chief of the Cahuillas, upon occasion of the recent disturbances. Its good results are already manifest; and it ought to be sustained by the community. Undoubtedly it will be sustained.

State of California—County of Los Angeles

Whereas Juan Antonio, Chief of the Cahuilla, and friend of the inhabitants of this county, as well as of all good and peaceable men has withdrawn from his residence in Apolitana, in consequence of a report that harm was meditated against him—which report is false—since he has always been considered in peace with all, and a friend of Order, he is hereby notified that he can return with his people to their homes, to live as before they left; take care of their property; work as they have always done; and associate with his white neighbors; with a guaranty [sic] that no harm shall be done him, either by individuals or by the county authorities, because all consider him as a good friend, and will not consent to let him be injured, but will cooperate with force if necessary, to punish any person who may disturb the peace.

In testimony thereof we subscribe our names at the rancho of San Bernadino, County of Los Angeles, this 2d day of June, 1851.

> Augustin Olivera, County Attorney
> Benjamin Hayes, County Attorney
> Ignacio Del Valle, County Recorder
> Stephen C. Foster, County Senator
> Diego Sepulveda, ranch of Yucaipa
> A. P. Hodges, Coroner
> Ignacio Palomares, rancho of San Jose
> E. H. M. Gower, Los Angeles
> H. R. Myles, Los Angeles
> Jose Del Carma Lugo, Justice of the Peace
> W. B. Osburn, Deputy Sheriff
> Montgomery Martin, Justice of the Peace
> D. G. Weaver, rancho of San Gorgonio

(As quoted in *Scrapbook of Benjamin Hayes*, Volume 38, Bancroft Library University of California, Berkeley.)

Los Angeles Star, July 19, 1851

An express sent to Juan Antonio, inviting him to meet the Commissioner at Chino, on a day named, and accordingly that chief and a large number of his warriors went to Chino where they remained five days, and were entertained by Col. Williams with the accostommed [sic] hospitality of a gentlemen. At the end of five days, Col. Barborer not meeting them, as agreed upon, the Indians returned to Apolitan, in no very good humor at the slight they had received. (As quoted in *Scrapbook of Benjamin Hayes*, Volume 38, Bancroft Library, University of California, Berkeley.)

Los Angeles Star, August 2, 1851

Juan Antonio, with about fifty of his people, arrived today from Apolitana. Some were mounted, some afoot, and all armed with bows and arrows, made quite a stir as they marched through Main Street to the Mayor's office. it appears that Juan Antonio had been told that the city was invaded by some bad men—(Wood and others)—and he forthwith brought his warriors to its protection. (As quoted in *Scrapbook of Benjamin Hayes*, Volume 38, Bancroft Library, University of California, Berkeley.)

Los Angeles Star, August 9, 1851

We alluded last week to the visit of the Apolitanas and their distinguished chief, Juan Antonio. They remained about town for three days, and then returned to Apolitan, having deported themselves with great propriety. One of their most solemn acts while in the city was the deposing of Juan Antonio, which was performed with some ceremony in the office of the County Judge. We know nothing of the causes which led to the result, but have been told that the Cahuilla regard Juan Antonio as unsafe—they say he is too head-strong. They elected as successor an Indian who received the approval and recommendation of the deposed captain. (As quoted in *Scrapbook of Benjamin Hayes*, Volume 38, Bancroft Library, University of California Berkeley.)

Los Angeles Star, November 1, 1851

Our city was disgraced on Saturday night by an affray which resulted in the killing of some half dozen Indians of the Cahuillas tribe and the serious wounding of as many more. It seems that on Saturday afternoon, Jose Antonio, the Alcalde of the Cahuilla long in this city, applied to the City Marshall for permission to play the Peon (a favorite game among the Indians) within the limits of the city. The Marshall refused, not only because the peon is prohibited by city ordinance, but because the Mayor had strictly charged him not to permit the playing of that game. The Alcalde then applied to Juan Sepulveda, one of the Justices of the Peace, who granted the request and detailed six Californians to act as a patrol, in order to prevent if possible, any disturbance on the occasion. Mr. Sepulveda, himself accompanied the patrol to the peon, which was held in front of the house of Jose Maria Ivarra, near the cemetery. During the evening an Indian known by the name of Cayote, who was trading for some liquor with Ivarra's wife, endeavored to take a bottle from her by force, but was prevented by Ivarra, who undertook to tie him in order to take him to jail. Five or six Indians interfered and rescued Cayote, and pulled Ivarra by the hair and abused him in other ways. The Indians then attacked the patrol, threw stones at them, and drove them up the hill and also threw a fire brand upon the house for the purpose of burning it and dared the Californians to an attack. Mr. Sepulveda, finding that he could not contend with the Indians, and that they appeared determined to burn the house, came down town for assistance and returned with seven Americans, among them Mr. Reeder, City Marshal, and Deputy Sheriff Osburn. When the party reached the ground, the Indians were on the side of the hill, whooping and yelling, and the Californians called to the Americans to come quickly to their aid. The Americans were armed, some with muskets and some with six shooters. Most of the Californians had swords. The Indians continued their endeavors to burn the house and were fired upon by the Americans and Californians. The firing was kept up for some five minutes, and until the Indians fled in all directions, the Californians pursued them. Twenty-one of the Indians took shelter in Ivarra's house, where they were captured and conveyed to the jail. (As quoted in *Scrapbook of Benjamin Hayes*, Volume 38, Bancroft Library, University of California, Berkeley.)

Daily Alta California, November 13, 1851

How many of the Indians were killed, is perhaps not positively known. Eight bodies were piled up before Ivarra's house. The number of Indians engaged in the affray must have amounted to nearly 100. The verdict of the Coroner's jury was that "the deceased came to their deaths while resisting the Sheriff's posse, and that the killing was justifiable."

The *peon* has always been a fruitful source of disturbance when held within the limits of the city, and it is only a few months since that it brought on an affray in which some five or six Indians were killed.

The Indians who were arrested on the occasion were taken before Justice Mallard, fined one dollar each, and sentenced to receive twenty-five lashes.

Los Angeles Star, November 1, 1851

Juan Antonio, the distinguished war chief of the Cahuillas, arrived in town yesterday with a party of his warriors, for the purpose of investigating the unfortunate occurrences of Saturday last. He is rigged out in epaulets, and other paraphernalia of military chieftains, and altogether has a martial bearing. Having succeeded in liberating those of his tribe who were confined in jail, he will immediately return to Apolitana. (As quoted in *Scrapbook of Benjamin Hayes*, Volume 38, Bancroft Library, University of California, Berkeley.)

Daily Alta California, June 17, 1851
Important from Los Angeles

The particulars of the destruction of the marauding party of Capt. Irving, consisting of himself and ten men, by the Indians, will be found fully detailed. Subsequent to that date an inquest was held upon the bodies, and after hearing a great deal of testimony, the coroner's jury returned the following verdict:

That the said John Irving, as well as ten others mentioned to wit: Odeneil, first name unknown, Hitchcock, first name unknown, George Bogoel, Frank Wilson, and six other persons whose names are unknown, and all of whose bodies were found on the ground near to the body of the said John Irving, came to their deaths on or about the 27th day of May, 1851, by the following cause, to wit: That said deceased on said day had broke into and robbed the houses of Jose Maria Lugo and Jose Carmel Lugo, in consequence whereof they were pursued by a party of Indians of the Cahuilla nation, whose aid had been sought by the owners of said houses and of the stolen property, and the said deceased were killed by said Indians, after being called upon to surrender themselves, and having refused so to surrender, to be dealt with according to law. We further find that the aid of said Indians was invoked on this occasion by Jose Carmel Lugo, as a citizen, for the protection of his own property; and that said Jose Carmel Lugo was a Justice of the Peace, and acted in the premises in that character. And we further find that the death of the said deceased is a justifiable homicide.

The following items of news we glean from the *Star.*

APOLITAN.— This rancheria is the residence of Juan Antonio, and his tribe of Cahuilla Indians, who killed Irving and his party on the 29th ult. It is situated on the rancho of San Bernadino. Juan Antonio has always been considered by the citizens of this county a well disposed and friendly chief. About eight years ago he was induced by the Mexican authorities of this county to settle at Apolitan to serve as a guard against the depredations of the horse stealing Indians, and land was furnished him by the owners of the rancho of San Bernadino. He has had written instructions from the Mexican authorities to kill Indian thieves and take away the stolen property. This authority was confirmed by Hon. Stephen C. Foster, acting as Alcalde of this District, and had been confirmed by all the previous local authorities The appointment was that of a general of the Cahuillas.

The Cahuillas are scattered in numerous rancherias along the mountains that bound this county. They number several thousand, and it is said that Juan Antonio can muster from twenty-five hundred to three thousand warriors.

A day or two after the massacre of Irving's band, a Sonorian went to Apolitan, and told Juan Antonio that two hundred men were on their way from Los Angeles with artillery, to take vengeance on the Indians. This alarmed them so much that they all fled to the mountains, and when the coroner went out he could not obtain an interview with Juan Antonio. The Indians fled in such haste that they lost two of their children, and for several days were unable to find them. Being assured that no harm would befall them, the Indians were subsequently induced to return to their rancherias.

Daily Alta California, June 3, 1851

The occurrences during the past month in this section of the State, have created serious apprehension in the minds of prominent citizens, that a political revolution will shortly take place in Lower California. The intelligence which I am about to communicate to you, is substantiated by the testimony of every respectable citizen of the southern portion of the State.

The condition of the country is alarming in the highest degree. It has for many months been held in complete subjection by bands of outlaws and highwaymen. These bands are composed generally of deserters from the United States army and other desperate adventurers, whose career commenced with the Mexican war, and who, after the treaty, came to this country ready for any deeds of robbery or blood. These bands had become the terror of the citizens of Los Angeles; they defied the laws; they robbed citizens in open day and with utter impunity; and finally, their chief, the noted John Irving, alias "Red Irving" formerly a Texan ranger, attempted to assassinate the Judge of the District Court in the public streets of the city. Such was the condition of things here, and the town, meantime, was in an entirely defence-less [sic] state. The command of Major General Bean was at this time encamped in the vicinity of Cajon Pass, sixty miles south of Los Angeles. I am not aware that a requisition was ever made upon General Bean by the civil authorities to protect the city. Though engaged in the most active and ardu-ous duties, and though the exigencies of the public service demanded that Gen. Bean and his corps should be concentrated around Cajon, he would have promptly responded to such a requisition had it been made.

The band, headed by Irving, after remaining here two months, started en route, as is believed, for Mazatlan. Before their departure they had, in the most ingenious manner, conveyed intelligence to the authorities of such a nature as they believed would cause the removal of Gen. Bean's command from the Cajon Pass. They were successful in their designs, and Gen. Bean sent off the principal part of his command to intercept a party of Indians whom Irving had induced the authorities to believe were engaged in robbing certain ranches. The object of Irving in deceiving the authorities and causing the removal of Gen. Bean's troops was avowedly to murder a family near the Cajon Pass, known as the Lugo family. Immediately after the departure of Bean's corps, Irving started from this city with his command, numbering as is supposed, forty men.

Shortly after his departure, letters were received in town from Col. Magruder, at Chino, and Mayor Wilson, of Los Angeles.

A meeting of the citizens was called, and it was determined to dispatch the sheriff, with a posse, to arrest Irving and his party, it being understood that the sheriff, on arriving at Cajon, should summon Gen. Bean's command to aid him in making the arrest. The sheriff started from the city with a large party of citizens, and on arriving at Cajon, was joined by Gen. Bean, with the remnant of his command remaining there. They started together in pursuit of Irving. That person had on the previous day detached eleven men from the main body of his party, and ordered them to follow him in the direction of Lugo's. The main body meantime proceeded on their journey with the understanding that Irving and his detachment would rejoin them after despatching [sic] the Lugo's. Irving arrived at the ranch, but the Lugo's hav-ing received notice of his intentions, had escaped, and were not to be found. Irving, doubtless exasperated at their departure, proceeded to plunder the ranch. He broke open trunks, forced doors, and destroyed and carried off various articles of value. He then, with his command, started to rejoin the main body. But he was not thus permitted to escape; he was doomed. The Indians attached to the rancheria in the vicinity, incited, I presume, by the

Lugo's, gathered in formidable numbers, and started in pursuit of Irving. Some of the Indians were well mounted, and all it is supposed, were well armed with bows and arrows and lances. Irving and his men were armed to the teeth, they carried Colt's revolvers and bowie's; but they were doomed. They repeatedly fired upon the Indians in pursuit without, as is supposed, killing or wounding any one of them.

Irving had proceeded in this way ten miles from the ranch, the Indians still continuing in close pursuit. At this distance from the ranch, he came to two roads, nearly similar in appearance, one being the main road, and the other a bye-road leading into a canada, or valley. Irving hesitated, faltered, and finally determined to take the bye-road, supposing, doubtless, that it would lead him safely through the mountains into a canada on the opposite side. This error was fatal to him and his command. No sooner had he taken the bye-road leading in to the Canada, than the Indians, numbering four or five hundred, closed upon him in the rear. Imagine the situation of that band of twelve men! In a mountain path just wide enough for two horsemen to ride abreast—on each side of these mountains ascending almost perpendicularly and so steep that horses could not scale them—behind them this body of Indians! Irving was deceived; the path or Canada did not lead to a valley on the opposite side; it led into a galob in the mountains from which there was not except by the path he was pursuing. As he proceeded at the head of his command, his situation became more apparent to him at every step of his progress. He could not turn back, and he went forward.

Daily Alta California, November 13, 1851
Southern Intelligence

Excitement at Los Angeles—A slip from the office of the Los Angeles Star, issued on the 26th ult, the day the Ohio left, furnishes us with the following information:

A company of men, numbering about forty, have been encamped near this city for some weeks past. They were commanded by Capt. Irving, a Texan, who proclaimed that he had been invited by the Governor of the State of Sonora, Mexico, to furnish aid to exterminate the Apaches. A number of depredations were committed while the company remained in this vicinity, and many people suppose that Irving's company is nothing more nor less than a band of robbers. Yesterday morning expressos reached this city from Col. Magruder, Capt. Lovell, and from several rancheros, giving information that Irving's company were moving down the valley, stealing horses, killing cattle, and conducting themselves in a most outrageous manner. They had threatened to ravish the females, and men, women and children had left the ranches, and fled to Gen. Bean's camp for protection. A meeting was held yesterday and the people stirred up to put an end to these outrages. Gen. Bean came in from the Cajon last evening. He will take the command of such force as can be raised in this city and at Chino, together with his own company. The forces are congregating at Chino. Our citizens are now mustering, and we judge, from the spirit manifested, that few prisoners will be taken. The whole county is arming, and in the event of a failure to arrest those marauders, an express will be sent to Major Hensly, at the Colorado.

A scouting party commanded by Dr. Hope, left Gen. Bean's camp about three weeks ago, intending to be absent for five days. They returned yesterday, and reported having had an engagement with the Pah-utahs, in which thirteen Indians were killed. Dr. Hope and his men, only five in number, were in natural fort, where they were attacked by the Indians, who gathered in great numbers. The Indians were driven from the fort, with the loss of thirteen of their number.

The Indians remained near the fort during [the] five days, and in such numbers that Dr. Hope's party deemed it dangerous to venture out. They had water in the fort, but suffered much from want of food; the Indians withdrew at the end of five days, and the party returned to camp. There was no water for many miles around, except in the fort, and it is presumed the Indians were compelled to give up the siege in consequence of the scarcity of water.

Private Gage received an arrow wound in the shoulder. No other person of the party was injured.

The natural fort above alluded to is about eighty miles beyond the Mohave, and is described as a most remarkable curiosity.

Dr. Hope came to town last evening.

Several persons who had been connected with Gen. Morehead's expedition, passed through this city on their way to the upper country, a few days since. They inform us that the expedition is bound to Sonora, in Mexico, where they will strike up a revolution. The armament of the Josephine consisted of two old muskets, but the General informed his men that he had a vessel ahead filled with fire arms and supplies. When the expedition reaches Sonora, we shall see "what we shall see."

Daily Alta California, December 1851
The Indian Troubles

The news from Los Angeles which we yesterday published, shows that a very alarmed and excited state of public feeling exists in that portion of the State, with regard to the probabilities of a general Indian outbreak, and somewhat tends also to modify the more pacific intelligence received from San Diego. The dates from San Diego are to the 7th inst., those from Los Angeles to the 30th ult. When these facts are taken into consideration, and the distance between the two points is allowed for, the two stories are easily reconciled, and it may therefore be very true that the whole rebellion has been quelled by the capture of Antonio Garra.

A careful examination of all the accounts, however, does not lead us to such a conclusion. It appears to us that the disaffection is much too widespread, and the preparations on the part of the Indians much too systematic and extensive, to be entirely overwhelmed by the capture of a single chief, though he may be the leader. And when is added to this the belief which has to some extent obtained, that the attack is instigated and urged on by the lower class of Californians, we are strongly impressed with the fear that the end is not yet.

The gentlemen in Los Angeles who have united to their exertions to procure men, arms, ammunition, etc., etc., are old residents in that section of the State. They know every inch of its territory, understand all its resources, and are intimately conversant with the number and character of its Indian tribes. These gentlemen tell us in plain language, and with the utmost deliberation, that they are in great danger. They say that many causes have conspired to render this revolt of the Indians more formidable, because more extensive, than any which has ever occurred. They give us the proofs that the combined Indian forces which will probably be brought against the whites extend in one unbroken and dangerous chain of tribes from Santa Barbara to the Rio Colorado.

It is, however, most gratifying in the present complexion of affairs, that the demand made upon the north is not for men. Fearful as they represent the perils which surround them, they do not exhibit unnecessary alarm. They appear to think themselves quite competent in numbers, if they had but the warlike instruments and munitions, to defend themselves against their wily and watchful enemy, if they do not succeed in ending the whole war by a sudden and spirited onslaught. That their prayer, in this particular, will be answered, there is little doubt. Certainly immediate steps should be taken to forward to Los Angeles a sufficiency of arms and munitions of war to answer every emergency which may arise.

We are among those who still consider the skies as overcast. Possessing no better means of information than the published accounts, we cannot find in them the reasons which would satisfy us that the difficulties are ended. Even admitting that the Indians have deserted Agua Calientes, and that the chief Garra is taken, if there be any foundation for the story of an Indian combination, those two occurrences would not necessarily end the war. If those accidents to the Indians should be followed up by active hostile demonstrations and subsequent successes on the part of the whites, the termination of the struggle might be speedily looked for; but if the rebellion exist in a tithe of the strength and extent the most reliable accounts would lead us to believe, nothing but a good sound drubbing of those engaged in it, and a severe example, will restore the southern country to a lasting peace and security.

Whilst we believe thus, it will but accord with our hopes to find that we have reasoned wrongly. We certainly trust that all the accounts may turn out to have been exaggerated—nothing would give us greater pleasure than to be found unnecessarily alarmed and over-credulous. But we anticipate no such gratification. The indications which we rely upon are much too unpromising and portentous.

Daily Alta California, December 1851
Latest from San Diego
Progress of the Indian War—Three Men Probably Hung!

By the arrival of the streamer Carolina, early this morning, we have dates from San Diego to the 10th instant. The favorable intelligence heretofore received appears to be borne out. We are indebted to the Parser of the Carolina for the annexed brief statement of the position of affairs when that vessel left:

On Tuesday, Dec. 9th, the Fitzgerald Volunteers returned to San Diego from an expedition against the Agua Caliente Indians, bringing three prisoners, two Indians and one American, named Bill Marshall. On the 10th, a court was convened and a jury appointed from the Fitzgerald Volunteers, to try the prisoners. Marshall was accused of having instigated the Indians to murder four Americans, and the Indians of being parties to the murder. At the time of our departure, the trial was not finished, but the general opinion was that the men would be condemned to death. The public feeling was very strong against the prisoners, and they would probably have been hung by the people had not the court been organised [sic]. A gallows was erected early in the morning, on the Plaza, for the purpose of executing them.

Daily Alta California, December 1851
Further Particulars of the Indian War in the South

We received yesterday, through the Post Office, the following detailed and interesting account of the military operations in the lower country, from our attentive and reliable correspondent:

SAN DIEGO, Cal., Dec. 9, 1851

GENTS:—The reports which you have received of the outbreak of the Indians have been confirmed. Yesterday the company of the "Fitzgerald Volunteers, " returned from the Aguas Calientes. The rancho of the Hon J. J. Warner had been burnt and sacked: the bodies of the four invalids (Hidgely, Fiddler, Black and Manning) found recognized. The Indians had assembled in the mountains at a place called *Coyotes*, in large numbers. The position occupied was inaccessible to any but foot men, and our command being too small (23 men) to divide, with nothing to eat for our animals, already worn out, all that could be done was to destroy their village and return for reinforcements.

Before reaching the Aguas Caliente, Capt. Fitzgerald despatched [*sic*] three Indians with a communication for Antonio. One of them returned next day and reported that chief absent from his command, and two days afterwards, with the renegades *Bill Marshall* and *Juan Bera*, and an Indian, reporting that Antonio Garra had been taken prisoner by Juan Antonio of San Bernadino, delivered to the authorities in Los Angeles, and that a general breaking up of the Indians had taken place in consequence of the loss of their head.

Last night a general meeting of the people was held in the Colorado House, and it was determined, unanimously, that as soon as the prisoners were brought in from the Mission, where they had been kept over night, they should be seized, a trial given them before the people assembled, and Marshall, (a white man) and Juan Bera, (a Californian) upon conviction, hung to the gallows the day before erected for them.

The Sheriff has resigned, (being a member elect of the Legislature) and in the absence of the County Judge; we are without a *single* civil officer in the county. These prisoners are now hourly looked for, and upon their arrival we shall see what we shall see. I may have time to give you the result of the action taken by the indignant populace, before the steamer leaves, for it will be short work after they are brought in. The Indian will probably be set free. This white man and the Californian were Antonio's advisers.

Too much credit cannot be given Major Fitzgerald and our worthy citizen and representative, Col. Haraszthy, who was 1st Lieut. of the company, for the zeal and activity manifest upon all occasions during their excursion, and for the manner in which this scouting party was conducted. They have thus expeditiously brought to an end a war that promised to harass not only the whole of the rancherias in this and Los Angeles county, but the cities also.

It has been reported that Capt. Harrison with his party of men, en route for the Colorado, had been attacked and destroyed. The report is not accredited.

Martial law has been revoked, though there is no civil law to the county, as I have stated, in consequence of the continued absence of the County Judge.

In haste, yours truly.

Daily Alta California, December 1851

I send you a hasty copy of the Sheriff's communication to the Governor. Yours truly,

The following is the communication of Mr. Harazthy, Sheriff of San Diego county, to Gov. McDougal:

SAN DIEGO CO., Nov. 26th, 1851

SIR: I have the honor to report to your Excellency that the Indian chief Capt. Antonio from Aguas Calientes, has commenced hostilities by attacking Hon. J. J. Warner's rancho, killing one of his servants, destroying his property, and driving off his stock. They killed on the same day, four Americans at Aguas Calientes, who went there to recruit their health. Said Antonio sent also a letter to Jose Antonio Estudillo (late Prefect) which is a formal declaration of war; the copy of which accompanies this. Receiving officially the above mentioned reports, I called on the captain of the organized Fitzgerald Volunteers, in which every able-bodied man had voluntarily enlisted, but the whole county not numbering over one hundred able-bodied men, destitute of arms, horses, &c., cannot do more than defend the city of San Diego, where an attack is daily expected. Apprehensive that some white men are united with the Indians, the citizens united in a mass meeting, and ordered the city and county under martial law. The force of Antonio is estimated at from 4 to 500 men; but as it is just concentrating, and the tribe can muster within three days at least 3,000 men, and Antonio having a large number of six shooters, rifles, and other arms, with the use of which his people are well acquainted, your Excellency will easily judge that our means are inadequate to resist a long time such a force.

I have to state further, that the Colorado Indians have arisen, killed four Americans, too the herd of sheep they drove, and attacked the military post at the Gila; in consequence of which all the available troops stationed at San Diego were ordered to the Colorado.

Therefore, in the name of the people of San Diego county, I respectfully request your Excellency's prompt aid and assistance, and to legalize, through your order, with further actions of the volunteers enlisted.

With pleasure I mention the fact that Major Fitzgerald, U.S.A., hearing the emergency, volunteered as a private, and deposited $120 out of his own purse for the purchase of provisions, &c., and in the same manner $500 have been collected from other good citizens.

Your Excellency will see from the above that we are in need of volunteers from other counties, as all of our county are on duty, and I fear Los Angeles county is in the same distress. Consequently, the quickest way would be to send a steamer from San Francisco with sufficient force, arms, &c. I also send a petition of the people of this county to Gen. Hitchcock.

> I remain, with high respect,
> Your most obedient servant,
> (Signed) Agoston Haraszthy.
> Sheriff of San Diego County

To his Excellency, Gov. McDougal.

The following is a communication of Antonio's referred to in the letter of Mr. Harazthy's:

Senor Don Jose Anto. Estudillo,—I salute you, the time I told you what I thought of things; now the blow is struck; if I have life I will go and help you, because all the Indians are invited in all parts, and it is possible that the San Bernadinos are now rising—and how a man by the name of Juan Berro told me that the white people waited for me, for this I give these my words, and to be prepared for Tuesday, to leave this for the Pueblo; and you will arrange with the white people and Indians, and send me your word, nothing more.

> (Signed) ANTONIO GARRA
> Agua Caliente, 21 Nov. 1851.
> A literal translation.

Daily Alta California, December 3, 1851
Important from the South
The Indians Rising—Attack on Warner's Rancho!—Departure of the Volunteers

We published on the arrival of the Ohio, the reports there in circulation through the southern country, in regard to the anticipated attack from the Indians. We have received the following communication from a friend in San Diego, by which it appears hostilities have actually commenced, and that the Indians are preparing for a determined warfare. We also publish the communication from Mr. Harazthy, Sheriff, to Gov. McDougal. The people of the south will probably require some assistance in the shape of arms and men:

San Diego, CAL., Nov. 28, 1851

Editors Alta:—San Diego county is in a blaze from the Colorado to the Pacific. The facts I shall notice in as brief a manner as possible. On the night of 22d inst., and a few hours after the arrival of the courier from the Colorado, of which I have already written you, another was received from Sta. Maria, stating that the Agua Caliente Indians, under their Chief Antonio, had arisen and destroyed the rancho of Hon. J. J. Warner. The day following the citizens enrolled themselves into a company of volunteers, for the purpose of proceeding to the seat of war; but finding much difficulty in procuring arms and ammunition, were delayed or unable to get off that day, and in the evening the Hon. J. J. W., himself appeared. He stated that he was in his house with only a crippled servant, (having that day sent his family off on suspicion), and found himself surrounded by Indians; several engaged in untieing [sic] three horses that were made fast to his door, whilst the others were robbing his corral of stock. He killed two, succeeded in getting one of the three horses, with his servant behind him, and left for a neighboring rancheria in a shower of arrows, none of which did him any injury.

The day following this, (24th), news came of the massacre of the invalids of the Aguas Calientes, four in number, the only names heard of are Ridgely and Slack. The succeeding day, (25th), received a letter from Antonio *declaring war*, if I may so term it; I enclose you a literal translation. He is said to be in command of not less than three thousand Indians, which he has been over twelve months organising [sic]; is now, and has done this within *sixty miles* of this town. He is allied with the Colorado Indians, and has invited the different tribes in Lower California and Los Angeles county to join him.

What now is the condition of the people of this county? In a few words, all the effective men, (and very few indeed) of the military command at this place, have gone to the relief of the detachment of troops at the mouth of the Gila: the whole country has concentrated at San Diego and formed themselves into a company which does not amount to fifty effective men: the town is under martial law, and all capable of bearing arms pressed into service for the protection of the town against an anticipated attack of hordes of Indians. Thus we now stand, with sentinels at every corner, business of all kinds suspended, easily stampeded, and scouts out to ascertain whatever facts they may be able.

Upon the call for volunteers, Maj. E. H. Fitzgerald, U.S.A., was among the first to enroll, and was unanimously proclaimed the captain, with power to appoint all of his officers. Through him and the zeal and co-operation of Bvt. Maj. Heintzelman, all have been furnished with arms and ammunition, which otherwise, for the want of these, would have placed the town in a very precarious situation. The whole number of men now in the county will not amount to *one hundred*, so we are utterly unable to do more than protect ourselves and families, though the company is ready to move in pursuit of Antonio as soon as his exact whereabouts is known. The facts have been represented to the Governor and General commanding in California.

The citizens express many obligations, and are under many, to Major Heintzelman, for the aid he has rendered them. I neglected stating that Warner's major-domo was killed, and burnt on his wood pile.

Believing the town to be secure, Capt. Fitzgerald leaves today with about 20 men of the volunteer company, for the Aguas Calientes, and I must be fixing my traps, or would enter more into detail.

Daily Alta California, December 4, 1851
The Southern Indian War

The intelligence which we gave in detail yesterday, through the attention of an esteemed friend at San Diego, narrating the actual commencement of hostilities by the savages in that region, has caused much excitement and great solicitude in our community. The defenseless condition of our fellow-citizens, their weakness in numbers, and their lack of provisions, have excited the unfeigned sympathy of our worthy inhabitants.

The position of our Southern friends appears extremely dangerous and imminent. Yet they have, with the courage and deliberation of true men, resolved to defend to the utmost their homes, property and the lives of those they most love. But they are almost powerless. They can muster but an hundred able-bodied serviceable men, against an Indian force of five hundred, already collected under that able leader, Antonio, with the almost certain prospect that the attacking force of the savages will be reinforced largely, perhaps as high as three thousand intelligent and energetic commander, but they are said to possess and understand the use of firearms.

The impression appears well founded that this attack of the Indians is but the precursor of a systematic and extended plan of operations against the whites, reaching from San Diego in the south, to Santa Barbara in the north. This conviction is so prevalent in all that region of the country, that the rancheros are removing their families and valuables into the towns as speedily as possible. That whole country is, therefore, in a most exposed, and perilous condition, without the men or other means to protect it against the inroads and depredations of the relentless savages.

In their extremity, the citizens of San Diego have declared the place under martial law, and formed a corps of volunteers. All business and industrial vocations have ceased, and uncertainty, alarm, and the sounds of martial preparation have taken the place of the peaceful and inviting scenes the same community presented but a week since. So obvious and imminent do the citizens consider their danger, that they have forwarded a petition to Gen. Hitchcock, commanding this division of the U.S. Army, for assistance of men and arms; and Sheriff Harazthy has written a letter to Gov. McDougal, recommending that the Executive at once take steps to dispatch a steamer with reinforcements for their relief.

Although we are anxious to believe that the anticipation of impending danger which our southern brethren entertain, are much exaggerated, we must confess they wear every appearance of probability. They appear of so imposing character, and are so borne out and consequent upon succeeding events, that there is no question but that it is the duty of the Commanding General of this Division, to take the proper and necessary measures in the premises; and we look with anxiety to see the matter proceeded upon with energy. If anything be done, it should be done at once. A day's delay, at the present critical conjuncture of affairs, may involve our friends in ruin and be followed with a long and bloody Indian war.

Should, however, the commanding officer of the U.S. forces not feel authorized to make any extraordinary exertions in this emergency, or should he not deem the occasion sufficiently imminent in its aspect to justify unusual proceedings, or should he not have at his command the necessary force for the purpose, we trust the Governor of the State will take immediate and efficient measures to organize a volunteer force and dispatch them to the aid of our beleaguered and periled fellow-citizens, together with such supplies as may be necessary and can be readily procured.

Most assuredly, the best course to legitimately, economically, and effectually accomplish the good work indicated, would be to leave it in the hands of army officers. But, if they be not inclined to enter upon the business, it appears to us that the promptings of a very ordinary humanity and sympathy render it obligatory upon the civil and military head of the State to take such a course as will evince his determination to use his powers for the protection and preservation of his constituents. So desirous is this community that our southern brethren should not be left without succor in their deep distress, that there is scarcely a doubt that five hundred volunteers could be raised here in a very few days, perhaps hours. Where patriotism, humanity, and duty point the way, who will be found wanting?

Daily Alta California, December 4, 1851
Matters in San Diego—Martial Law Proclaimed

In addition to our Southern correspondence published yesterday, we have received a copy of the San Diego Herald, of the 27th ult., through the politeness of Mr. J. Figel, which contains a later account of the condition of affairs in and about that place, and announces that the city has been placed under martial law. Says the Herald—

Our citizens have for some weeks past apprehended trouble with the Indians, and on Monday morning last assembled in town meeting and proclaimed martial law—the following among other reasons, influencing this course of conduct. The County Judge (Hays) has been absent from his post many months, and in consequence of his absences, our newly elected Justices of the Peace are unable to qualify— leaving us almost entirely deprived of proper legal authority. Again, a portion of the native Californians were backward in volunteering to the circumstances, to bring them under strict military discipline.

The same paper also says:

The town now presents the appearance of a fortified camp. Sentinels on duty at every approach to the city are "pacing their lonely round," no Indian being permitted to pass without giving a good account of himself. The Mayor of San Diego, recognizing the people as the exponent and origin of all law, quietly acquiesces in what has been done by his constituents, and has patriotically enrolled himself as a member of the Volunteer company on duty in our city.

The Herald publishes the letter from Antonio Garra, which we gave yesterday, and comments as follows:

We invite attention to the letter written by Antonio Garra, the chief of the principal tribe of Indians, to Don Jose Antonio Estudillo, one of our most respected citizens. This letter, together with some other circumstances that have come to light, has induced the belief that some of the abandoned of the native population are co-operating with the Indians. The writer, Antonio Garra, received a tolerable Spanish education at the Mission of San Luis Rey, and is regarded by all who know him, as a man of energy, determination and bravery. As one of the principal chiefs his power and influence over the Indians is almost unbounded. Since the Sheriff of this county (most unwisely, in our judgment) attempted to assess and collect a tax on his cattle, Antonio has exhibited the most malignant feelings toward our government, and has been busy for weeks past in dispatching couriers to the different tribes, inciting them to hostilities, and offering a co-operation on his part. The dark war-cloud that has so long hovered over us, has burst, spreading terror and dismay throughout this wide-spread and thinly populated country. The ball is in motion, and unless the most active steps are taken by the government at once, a protracted, ruinous and vexatious war is before us, involving in its prosecution many valuable lives, and the expenditure of many millions of money. Unlike the Indians of the North, our foes are a fighting people, not unacquainted with the use of firearms, and possessing some property, with an immense extent of country on the Gila and beyond its confines, to which they can flee for security in case of being hard pressed.

We quote the annexed items from the same paper which publishes the above; premising, however, that in the excitement represented, much needless alarm may perhaps be felt:

ALARMED—The people resident on the ranches south and east of this city, becoming alarmed at the hostile feelings exhibited by the Indians are flocking to our town for protection.

ALARM OF THE MISSION INDIANS—A gentleman direct from San Luis Rey, informs us that the Indian residents of *Temacata*, a village situated at the base of the mountains, twenty five miles east of the Mission of San Luis, and on the emigrant road leading from Warner's to Los Angeles, are moving their families and stock to this city; their chief, Pablo, having declined to join Antonio in his foray against the whites. Pablo is an educated Indian, the owner of a fine rancho and large herds of cattle. He may be expected here this evening. The entire country is alarmed, and without prompt assistance from the North, our situation in a short time may become critical.

Daily Alta California, December 10, 1851
Letter From San Diego

Through the attention of Purser Poole of the steamer Pacific, we have received intelligence from San Diego to the 7th inst.

Col. Hooper arrived from Agua Caliente just before the Pacific sailed from San Diego, and reported that the Indian chief Antonio Garra, who is the principal instigator of the outbreak against the whites, had been captured by Juan Antonio, the chief of the Wiscole, and carried to Los Angeles.

The Volunteers from San Diego had found and buried the bodies of the four Americans who were murdered at Agua Caliente. The Indians had fled from that place—probably in the consequence of the seizure of their chief—and the volunteers were returning to San Diego.

Information had reached San Diego that Bill Marshall, (a white man) Juan Berno, and several other instigators of the revolt, were at Santa Maria, and the Sheriff with an armed posse of twelve men had gone to arrest them.

The tenor of this intelligence is decidedly favorable, and if it be true, of which there appears but little doubt, a South will fortunately be spared that horrors of a bloody Indian war.

Daily Alta California, December 12, 1851
Later from the South—The Indian War

The brig Fremont arrived yesterday from San Pedro, bringing several days later intelligence from the seat of Indian difficulties.

Mr. Ferrell, Collector for the port of San Diego, came up in the Fremont, bearer of dispatches to Gov. McDougal from Gen. Bean.

Below will be found an extract from the Governor's dispatches, for the [perusal] of which we are indebted to his Excellency.

The only assistance which the South requires, it will be seen by these papers, and by the letter of our attentive correspondent, is of means and munitions of war. At the latest date of our advices [sic], Nov. 30th, the inhabitants of Los Angeles county were preparing to proceed against the allied Indian forces, and it was thought by them that with a supply of ammunition and arms they could very well put down the insurrection. They have chosen a Board of War Commissioners, and are collecting animals at a pace of rendezvous, on which to mount an expedition of two or three hundred men, who will thenceforth proceed against the Indians. Gen. Bean, who was in Los Angeles, solicits of the Governor arms and ammunition for the companies already raised.

The following is the extract from the dispatches received yesterday, dated Los Angeles, Nov. 30th:

An examination of our means of defence [sic] exhibits an alarming state of weakness. This proceeds, not from a want of men, but of arms. We are without guns, pistols, or any of the proper arms for cavalry, which alone can conduct effective war upon the hostile tribes of savages that are devastating our country.

The United States have a company of infantry consisting of about thirty men, at Chino, about thirty miles from this place. They are unable to render any assistance, as they are not mounted, nor have they suitable arms, and are short of ammunition. I am therefore thrown for resources entirely upon the patriotism of the citizens, and cannot but bear cheerful testimony to the prompt manner in which they are responding to the emergency. Owing to their voluntary and praiseworthy generosity, there is no lack of means to get supplies; but the great and almost insurmountable difficulty is want of arms. All the blacksmiths have been set to making laces for the Californians.

Representing these facts, therefore, I urgently call the attention of the commander-in-chief to our want of arms and accoutrements [sic]. We want six abooters or holster pistols, sabres [sic], carbines and rifles. If they are sent immediately it may save the State hundreds of thousands as by enabling us to strike a quick and effective blow, the war may be suppressed before it has broken out far and wide.

Two, and perhaps three companies of cavalry will leave this place to march against the Aguas Calientes Indians in a few days. They will be chiefly composed of native Californians and resident citizens, who are leaving their ordinary avocations at a great sacrifice. If the Indians of the rivers Gila and Colorado should destroy the United States troops and ferrymen, they would probably form a junction with the Aguas Calientes and Cahuilla Indians. If this junction should be effected, it would present an Indian force of four or five thousand warriors. It would strain the energies of the county to their utmost tension to resist so formidable a combination, if it could be resisted at all.

Through the politeness of Mr. Ferrell we have been placed in possession of the following letter from an American gentleman of standing in that section of the State. Without vouching for its correctness, we think it more just to all parties that it should be published—

Los Angeles, Nov. 30, 1851.

GENTLEMEN:—I hasten to apprise you of the condition of our affairs, and lay before you our prospects under the pressure of the Indian difficulties.

The great cause of alarm and apprehension here is that we have not adequate means of defence [sic] against a powerful foe. They do not exist in Southern California.

The county of Los Angeles will be able to send out a company of about seventy-five Americans and fifty Californians, and so great is the apathy of the Californian part of the population, that horses must be pressed into the service and provisions taken where they can be had. We have reason to believe that many Californians of the baser sort are in secret combination with the Indians.

We are also nearly destitute of arms. There is not a cannon in this county, and as for muskets, there are not more than eighty good, bad, and indifferent, in the county, except with the twenty U.S. soldiers at the Rancho del Chino. NO small arms can be had, and there are but few in the county in the hands of private individuals. There is only but 300 lbs of powder in the stores for sale, and but little lead. Thus you see how poorly supplied with arms and ammunition we are. However, we shall do our best to meet the crisis as

Americans, proud of the name, and conscious of the high character of our birth right.

It cannot be disguised that there is an Indian war against Americans, solely. Almost the whole California population is disaffected with our *institutions*—or, you may change the word, and say our *tax system*. Fond of changes—used to *"revolucion"* every two years, they are restive under our system. And although you will see by the "Star," that Andreas Pico has promised fifty Californians for the war, yet the common people among them say none will go without being *forced*. There are undercurrents at work here, which I have not time to explain, but which point to but one common cause—a deep, deadly hatred in the minds of the lower order of the native Californians against the Americans. The smothered fire is breaking out in a general Indian war, excited, as Indians themselves say, by California emissaries.

Already, the laws cannot be enforced against any Californians of influence. Although the Sheriff, with several posses, has endeavored to arrest some of the Lugos under a bench warrant he is unable to do it, for the fact that they range from ranch to ranch, over an immense area, secreted by their "parientes" and "compadres." To arrest those who secrete them, as accessories after the fact, would fill our jail with most venerable old men, women, and young men, and produce at once war to the knife, and from the knife to the hilt, between Californian and American. There are a few well disposed and respectable Californians, who are with us here, for a faithful execution of the law; but they do not act, from terror inspired by the bad. The Sheriff has been resisted with overpowering force, the secret work of assassination is commenced, and an Indian war is upon us, all at the same moment. It is said that Solomon Pico ranges with impunity in our country, secreted by the rancheros; and if his own countrymen are to be believed, he is an "incarnate devil." That he was concerned with the Lugos in the attempt to assassinate Benjamin Hayes, is generally conceded by Californians. But the officers of the law, although they use all their energy, must be powerless under such circumstances to bring offenders to justice.

Col. Ferrell, of San Diego, is bearer of dispatches from Gen. Bean to the Governor, and you will obtain valuable information from him as to the real state of things in this part of the State. I write by him.

In haste yours, PHILO.

San Diego Herald, January 17, 1852.
Trial of Antonio Garra, the hostile Indian Chief

A militia court Martial, consisting of Maj. Gen. Bean, Maj. M. Norton, Maj. Santiago E. Arguello, Lt. Hooper, and Lt. Titghman, assembled on the 8th inst. for the trial of Antonio Garra. The Court met pursuant to orders, whereupon Capt. Cave J. Couts was appointed Judge Advocate, hon. J. J. Warner, interpreter Maj. McKinstry, U.S.A., at the request of the Court and prisoner, consented to act as counsel for Garra. The prisoner was then arraigned on the following charges:

1st. TREASON.—*Specification,* That he, Antonio Garra, did levy war against the State of California, this during the months of November and December, 1851, at and in the vicinity of Agua Calientes, county San Diego, State of California.

Charge 2d. MURDER.—*Specification,* That the said Antonio Garra did aid and order the attack of the Agua Calientes and Warner's Rancho, on or about the 23d of November 1st, resulting in the killing of Ridgely and others.

Charge 3d. ROBBERY.—*Specification first,* That Antonio did aid and abet the stealing of certain stock, cattle, &c., from the rancho of J. J. Warner, and in burning his house, destroying property, household furniture, &c., to a large amount; this on or about 23d of Nov. 1851. *Specification second,* That said prisoner did aid and abet in robbing , and stealing a certain number of sheep, at or near the Rio Colorado from a party of Americans, most of whom were murdered to accomplish the robbery; this on or about November, 1851, county San Diego State of California.

To all of which, the prisoner plead as follows:

Charge and specification 1st, Not Guilty.

Charge and specification 2d, Not Guilty.

Charge and specification 3d, Not Guilty.

Specification 2d of charge 3d, Guilty.

Hon. J. J. Warner, witness for prosecution, swore, testifies as follows:

That he knows of nothing that can tend to terminate the prisoner of the charges of treason, but all I do know of him as regards the charge, is that war has been levied; but as far as concerning the prisoner, I know nothing. On Saturday morning, Nov. 23d, about sunrise, I was awoke by the war-whoop, and having had cause to suspect, I ran to the door and met my Indian boy who said, the Cahuillas are on us, and then I saw two horses made fast and which they succeeded in getting loose, and upon presenting myself at the door, gun in hand, immediately they secreted themselves, when I succeeded in killing one, and shortly afterwards shot another, while running from my house to an outhouse. Near me were at least twenty Indians. There was no person in my house but myself a sick mulatto boy and an Indian boy. I returned to the house and procured another gun, and succeeded in getting a horse saddled, and made my Indian boy an inter-preter to inquire of them what they wanted, and he ran away and joined them. I then returned to my house and found it stripped of everything, but the Indians had all retired. The great body of them, I think, were about two miles off. While riding I overtook an Indian who had some of my property, when I ordered him to return them to my house, he dropped his load and attempted to draw an arrow, when I shot him. I was subsequently one of a number who were at Agua Calientes, and there I saw the bodies of Ridgely, Slack, and Fidler, and although they were much disfigured, yet I recognized them. My work horses were not stolen, neither were my breeding mares, that day. There must have been some 100 or 150 Indians. "Can you give the names of any Indian or Indians who made the attack upon your house?" "No." "Do you know Juan Baptista?" "I do." "Were you fired upon first?" "I was." "Were any mounted?" " None that I saw." "Who is looked upon as chief of the party that made the attack on your house?" "Antonio Garra. I know nothing further of the Agua Calientes murder, except that I saw the dead bodies. I believe those who attacked me are of the San Louis Rey Indians, of whom the prisoner is chief."

Antonio Garra was then questioned, and said that the Indians who attacked Warner's rancho were of the tribe of Cahuillas. He was asked why he stopped at San Tsicho when his people went to Agua Calientes and killed the Americans; to which he replied, that he was sick, but the Cahuillas forced him to go: that he never ordered nor commanded that with which he was charged. "When you stopped at San Tsicho did you ask Bill Marshall and Juan Bero if the Cahuillas were coming?" "Yes, but they did not come by my orders. 'Why,' said they, 'are you going to back out now that everything is arranged?' "When you were asked, 'why do you not go with us, now that you are compromised?' what did you say?" "I replied, 'You do this to have the blame laid upon me, but I have done nothing to do with it.'"

The Court then adjourned til 4 o'clock, when the Hon. J. J. Warner was called upon to testify in relation to the other matters of little interest.

Maj. McKinstry, by request, gave his opinion that the prisoner could not be legally tried on a charge of treason, whereupon the Court adjourned, to meet next day at 9 A.M.

9 A.M., Jan. 10. Session resumed. Present all the members.

Pedro Carillo sworn as interpreter. The Judge Advocate, then announced that he would read the confession of Bill Marshall. The Court deemed it unnecessary to multiply evidence, therfore the reading of the confession was dispensed with.

Lieut. Hamilton sworn.—I was a member of a council of war that investigated the Indian difficulties. Francis Necate testified before that tribunal, that Antonio Garra visited his house on the evening before the murder of the Americans at Agua Caliente. He sent for Bill Marshall and Juan Bero and some others. Bill and Bero answered the summons. Antonio Garra then ordered the murder of the Americans at Agua Caliente. He sent for Bill Marshall and Juan Bero and some others. Bill and Bero answered the summons. Antonio Garra then ordered the murder of the Americans at Agua Caliente. Bill and Bero started to carry the order into execution. Garra did not appear to have confidence in them and directed an Indian named Jacobo to follow them and see that his orders were properly executed.—Jacobo retired and returned early next morning, and reported to Garra that the Americans had been killed. He also stated, that during that night Garra had issued orders to attack Warner's ranch, and threatened to kill any one who failed to comply with his orders. The order was executed with the assistance of Panito and Razon's people, Chapule directing the attack. Jacobo, when examined, denied the statements of Francisco, and said that Garra did all in his power to prevent the murders, but was too late. The Council of War, however, convicted Jacobo of being a participator in both affairs. Louis, the Alcalde of Agua Caliente, testified before the same tribunal, that Antonio visited his house on the night of the murders, and told him that it was his father's orders that the Americans should be killed; that no one need entertain fears about assisting him (Antonio), because he and his father would take the responsibility. Three other witnesses testified to the same thing. Francisco denied all knowledge of Garra's plans for carrying on the war. He sated, that after the commission of the murders Garra gave orders to his people to flee to the mountains. The following morning, Jacobo returned and asked the people why the murders had been committed. They replied that such a question came with a good grace from him. Jacobo said that the orders were to flee to some remote point. Antonio's heart failed him previous to the attack on Warner but Panito stated that they had assembled for that purpose, and that they would do it whether Garra directed it or not. This was on the 23d of November. The Council of War was held at the Cayotes on the 23d of December. There were no papers found at the Cayotes, except a few old Mexican patents—nothing was found tending to criminate anyone.

Gen. Bean was sworn for the dense, after which Major [McKinley] addressed the court in a long and able argument, denying the right of the Court to take cognizance of the offenses charged against the prisoner, and contending that it was an absurdity so glaring, that he trusted the Court, in deference to their own standing as sensible men, would throw out the charge of Treason. That the prisoner owed no allegiance to the State of California, and therefore, under no circumstances, could be guilty of the crime of treason. He claimed that the prisoner was a prisoner of war, and adduced an array of authorities in support of the position he had assumed, and in conclusion demanded, in the name of an outraged community, that Mr. Ortega should be confronted with the prisoner, who desired to make certain revelations seriously affecting that gentleman.

The Court was then cleared for deliberation, and found the prisoner guilty of *murder* and *theft*, and sentenced him to be shot to death.

THE EXECUTION

Antonio Garra, the Indian chieftain, who was convicted of murder and theft, before the Militia Court Martial, of which Gen. Bean was President, was executed pursuant to his sentence, on Saturday evening last. About 3 o'clock on the afternoon of that day, it was officially announced to him that he must die, and Padre Juan remained with him from that time till the moment of his death. At half past 4, the preparations for his death being completed, the execution party, ten in number, commanded by Capt. G. B. Fitzgerald, paraded before the cell of the condemned, and the Provost Martial announced to Antonio that his hour had come. The prisoner took his place at the head of his executioners, and marched to his grave, evidently determined to show his captors that an Indian brave could die like a man. No unbecoming levity marked his conduct, but his whole deportment evinced the brave man prepared to meet his fate. Upon arriving at his grave, the prisoner placed himself at its head, and only after the repeated solicitations and commands of his father confessors was he induced to ask pardon of the large crowd assembled, which he did after his own manner.—Lifting his eyes, with a smile denoting contempt, he said in a loud and clear tone, devoid of all tremor, "Gentlemen, I ask your pardon for all my offenses, and expect yours in return." Then suffering his eyes to be bandaged, he kneeled at the head of his grave, when the Provost Marshall, turning to his troops, commanded Ready? Aim? Fire? The sun's last rays were at this moment lingering on the hills of Point Lobos, whilst the bells of the neighboring church chimed vespers. In an instant, the soul of a truly "brave" winged its flight to the regions of eternity accompanied by the melancholy howling of dogs, who seemed to be aware of the solemnity of the occasion—casting a gloom over the assembled hundreds, who, whilst acknowledging the justness of Antonio's fate, failed not to drop a tear o'er the grave of a brave man and once powerful chieftain.

Mission of San Diego California
August 23, 1856

Sir,

Thomas, the principal Captain of the Santa Isabel Indians, together with thirteen of his Captains came into this post some two weeks since, and complained that Mr. J. J. Warner, (Sub Agent for these Indians) had informed them of his intention to take all animals, having no brands upon them, in the hands of the Indians, from them as his property.

As many of these Indians own mares, which have had colts, and which are not branded for the reason that they have no brands, this proceeding would be manifestly unjust. I therefore directed Thomas to bring the animals here in case any attempt was made to take them, and I would endeavor to secure his property for him.

This is one of the many cases of injustice practiced upon these Indians, and by the very men whose duty it is to protect them, and I presume my action will be reported as "an interference on the part of the military" with the duties of an Agent. I therefore have the honor to report the case, in order that the Commanding General may be made aware of the characters of the persons making such reports.

I am Sir,
Very respectfully,
Your obt. Servt.
Wm. A. Winder
1st Lt. 3 Arty.
Comdg. Post

To
Bvt Major W. W. Mackall
Asst Adjt. General
No. 61. Dept. Pacific Div.
Benicia Cal.

(National Archives, Records of the War Department, Record Group 98, Letters Received, Department of the Pacific, 1856, Box 5, Document W104, as quoted in *The Destruction of California Indians*, p. 105.)

★★

Chapter 5

ANGLO DEPREDATIONS AGAINST CALIFORNIA INDIANS

The Gold Rush brought a tide of people from all over the world to California. Thousands from the United States—mostly men—soon arrived in the region. Anglos carried with them dangerous attitudes toward North American Indians. For centuries, the English and their American descendants drove Indian peoples from their indigenous homelands. Whites indiscriminately killed Native Americans, considering native people to be less than human. This legacy of hatred and murder continued in California during the Gold Rush.

Many whites viewed the indigenous inhabitants of the Golden State as obstacles to their economic well-being. Beginning in 1849, with the attack on a Maidu village, American military units, militia groups, and vigilantes fought Indians in what essentially became a war of extermination. For instance, whites organized the Mariposa Battalion for the sole purpose of killing Indians in the Southern Mines. Many Anglos preferred to kill Native Americans rather than remove them to federal reservations. They hunted down and mercilessly murdered Indian men, women, and children—sometimes hundreds at a time. At least one newspaper correctly described the murders as "wholesale killing." Another document relates how white men brutally slit the throat of a crippled Indian boy. The courageous lad had attempted to defend a little girl from the Anglo intruders. Miners raped Indian women and enslaved children, forcing young girls into prostitution or selling them outright to the highest bidder.

Several newspaper articles in this chapter seek to justify the abundant Indian murders committed by whites. Many journalists first detail Indian raids on "innocent" American communities and then recount how whites "retaliated" only as a defensive measure. Anglos assumed that they could kill any Indians, even those not involved in raids against whites. In the eyes of Americans, murdering Indians became a crusade—a righteous, noble act. The press thereby strives to convince readers that these killings are just and Native Americans simply got what they deserved. In fact, these accounts attempt to blame native people for their own deaths.

Daily Alta California, June 2, 1849
From the **Placer Times** of May 12

CORRECT DETAIL OF THE MASSACRE OF INDIANS ON GOSUMNE RIVER-STATEMENT OF WM. DAYLOR.—The letter below was received at our office shortly after our own prepared account had been published. In many particulars it will be found to differ materially from the one referred to. We readily give it a place.

"On about the 20th ult. I left my rancho with a party of Indians in my employ for the mines. After making such arrangements as were necessary, I left them and returned. About the 26th a party of armed white men came to their camp, or where they were at work, and killed an Indian while working with a crow-bar, and on his knees; they then shot another through the arm, who tried to escape. After a run of a short distance he was shot through the thigh, when trying to conceal himself, his brains were beat out with rocks and stones. Some white men who were about my camp, on hearing the alarm ran towards the spot and met the party coming back, who warned them not to go further, the Indians were fighting, they said. They minded them not, but proceeded to where they found the bodies of the slain Indians, the remainder of the party having fled. The company of whites now followed on the trail of the Indians, and about ten miles from my house overtook a party traveling to their home, and surrounded them without difficulty; in a few moments commenced separating the men from the women and children, when apprehending danger, the men broke and attempted to escape. Three were allowed to get off, the rest, fourteen in number, were slaughtered on the spot. The same day, or next, about noon, the party of whites arrived and encamped about 150 yards from my house. Myself, wife and cousin were about to bury a member of the family, deceased, and previous to leaving the ground, I was informed that a party of armed men were at the house and about to kill the Indians there. I returned with my wife, and a few moments after, the four Indians left the grave and passed within thirty steps of the camp when they were fired upon, and one fell dead, another passed not ten steps from my door, wounded, the remaining two escaped. The captain of the company of white men came to my house shortly after and requested me to kill a beef for his men; I refused, and they soon after raised camp. The next morning, I was called by my wife to see two men who were riding rapidly to the south; in a few moments they wheeled and galloped hard back. Then I saw Indians running to take shelter in the brush. I sent for them and they came and told me that a party of white men had taken a small party of women and children prisoners. Where, or for what purpose, I am unable to say. I, with four Indian servants, buried 15 Indians, slain, and found the remains of one partly burned. Mr. Thos Rhodes, with the assistance of two or three Indians, buried the bodies of the first two killed. The white men report having killed 27 before coming to the house. Twenty-two men, and thirty-four women and children are yet missing from the rancheria."

W M. DAYLOR

Daily Alta California, January 26, 1851
Correspondence of the Daily Alta California

Near CASTORIA, Jan. 21, 1851

MESSRS. EDITORS: I informed you on the 14th inst. that Savage had started on the 8th from Agua Frio, with 300 men, to attack the Indians, who had of late committed depredations between the Tuolumne and Maraposa [sic]. I have just heard that Savage has been defeated, and has returned. He lost two men. At the last accounts he was endeavoring to raise a force of 600 men. He informed the people that the Indians had 500 or 600 head of horses and mules, and 400 or 500 head of oxen, which would pay them, in case they received nothing from the government. I have heard no further particulars.

The expedition from the Mokelumne against the Indians was successful. The Indians ran off, leaving behind them all their arms and plunder. It is said that the Frenchmen who went on the expedition, found rich diggings, in the Indian country, on one of the Forks or tributaries of the Stanislaus. A tin cup of earth yielded two dollars. They have remained in the mountains.

Daily Alta California, January 26, 1851
San Joaquin Intelligence
Castoria Correspondence
Savage's Engagement with the Indians—His Second Expedition—Massacre of Thirteen Whites on Four Creeks—Shocking Reports, &c.

NEAR CASTORIA, Jan. 22, 1851

MESSRS. EDITORS: I have just received the particulars of Savage's late engagement with the Indians. With some fifty men, he approached in the night to within sixty or eighty yards of the Indians' camping ground, where he remained in ambuscade, intending to make an attack at daybreak. He was discovered, however, by the Indians, and on hearing the alarm in their camp, he thought it best to discharge upon them, which he did. The chief threw up his arms as Savage implored him not to fire, assuring him that they wished to make peace. Savage's men, however, fired, and the Indians retreated into the bushes. They soon rallied again, and fought the whites almost hand to hand, drove the Indians from the ground, and destroyed ten or fifteen tons of dried meat. Savage had one man killed and three wounded. A number of Indians fell. The Indians informed Savage that they would meet him on Sunday, the 19th. He retired five miles from the ground, built a fort, left his men in it, and went to Agua Frio and Burns' for reinforcements. On Thursday or Friday last he left with two hundred men for the mountains. Savage has lost all goods he had at his principal trading post, and all his animals except three or four mules. He offers $250 reward for the recovery of a favorite mule. He has some goods on the Mariposa.

On Thursday evening last, news was received at Burns', from Fine Gold Gulch, 60 miles south, of the massacre by the Indians of all the settlers on Four Creeks, some hundred and fifty miles south of Burns'. Three men who had been prospecting on Owen's Lake found the cabins and tents on Four Creeks burnt, and the bodies of thirteen white men on the ground, with the entrails torn out! One was the body of Mr. Cassidy, of Louisiana.

About a week since, all the settlers (eighteen) on Solomon's Gulch, two and a half miles above Ridley's Ferry, on the Mercede [Merced], were missing, and it is feared they have been killed by Indians.

There are some shocking reports from Rattlesnake Creek, but as I have heard them contradicted I will not give particulars.

R. W.

Daily Alta California, January 29, 1851
Castoria Correspondence
The Indian Outbreak on the Mariposa—Murder of three Whites and Destruction of Savage's Camp—Savage's First Expedition against the Indians—The Indian Strong Hold—The Battle—Twenty-seven Indians and two Whites killed—Destruction of the Indian Camp and Provisions— Incidents of the Battle—Seven Whites Murdered—Life and Character of Savage—His Second Expedition—Burns' Diggings—Situation of Miners- Quartz Vein Discoveries.

Near Castoria, Jan. 27, 1851
Messrs. Editors: As there were some few errors in my recent accounts of the Indian troubles in the South, allow me to give you a correct statement of all that has occurred, down to the latest advices [*sic*].

About three months since, Jim Savage moved from the Frizno, a small stream, thirty miles S. E. of the Miraposas [Mariposas], where he had a store, and established a trading post on the Miraposas [sic], and one at Burns', 25 miles this side of the Miraposas [sic]. He was at Burn's [sic] recently, when his two squaws were taken off, and he was informed by Indians that his three men at Miraposas [sic] had been murdered, his goods carried off and his camp burnt. He immediately went to Miraposas [sic], and found that the report was true. He had lost about $8,000 worth of goods.

Being acquainted with the Indians' stronghold in the mountains—a hollow place, surrounded by precipices, timber, and chapparel [sic], and accessible only through a narrow pass—he raised a company of forty-three men, and left Mariposa on the 7th instant, for the Frizno, where they built a log fort and left their animals, provisions, and four men. They traveled afoot sixty miles, and arrived in the vicinity of where they supposed the Indians were camped, on the evening of the second day. Savage went ahead, and discovered the retreat of the Indians. They were carousing around large fires, talking loud, eating, dancing, gambling, &c. Savage could learn from what was said, that they expected an attack from the Americans. The night was spent in clambering over rugged mountains. Towards morning, a charge was made upon the Indian camp, through the narrow pass. The Indians fled into the thickets, but soon rallied, and crowded so closely upon the whites, and in such numbers, that the latter thought it prudent to retreat into some timber, and take shelter from the arrows. There were eight or ten rifles and pistols among the Indians; but the whites had the advantage, and so many Indians fell that they retreated. Savage's party then set fire to the camp, and destroyed some sixty or seventy huts, a large American tent, and an immense quantity of mule meat and acorn meal. The huts were covered with mule meat, and the acorn meal was hung in baskets to the trees. Twenty-seven Indians were killed. Two Americans, named Little and Sylvester were killed. One, named Richard Rillotson, from New York State, had his nose shot off with a rifle ball, and was wounded with arrows. An old squaw, who fought well, and was wounded in the affray, was burnt with the camp.

It was stated in the Stockton papers that the Mexican who was with Marianna when he murdered Savage's partner, Foster, had been shot by a friend of Foster. I am assured by Mr. J. M. Hogan, of New Orleans, who was one of Savage's party, that Savage recognised [sic] this Mexican and another among the Indians. He stood out boldly, and exchanged two or three deliberate shots with Major Burney. The Major thinks he shot him through the shoulder. Foster's revolver, found where the murder was committed by Marianna, and taken from Savage's camp on the Mariposa, was found by

Savage in the Indian camp. During the skirmish the Indians called for Savage to "come out," and several of them rushed recklessly among the Americans, calling for Savage, that they wanted to kill him. He was disguised, however, so that they did not recognise [*sic*] him. It was supposed that there were three or four hundred Indians on the ground. The chief informed the whites that three hundred of their warriors were absent on an expedition to the settlements, but they would meet them again. This statement has been confirmed by the fact, that about this time seven whites were killed at the Red Banks, on the Mercede [Merced], and sixty mules were taken from Hill's, and sixty from Hoard's rancho, on the Mercede [Merced]. Eleven other men are missing from Red Banks.

Savage is a man possessing more than ordinary intelligence and shrewdness, He is about twenty-eight years old, and remarkable for his energy of character, and whole souled [*sic*] generosity. He is of German descent, and from Illinois, where he went to school until he was fourteen, when he became a mountaineer, and lived several years among the Sacs and the Foxes, and other Indians. Five or six years ago he came to this county, and has lived mostly among the Indians, over whom he has had the control of a chief, until recently. He speaks five Indian tongues, besides German, French, Spanish, and English.

He has started on a second expedition with a larger force. There is a report of his having defeated the Indians, killed three hundred, and taken one hundred and fifty squaws—but it needs confirmation. His uniform when he left Mariposa was a tattered coat, corderoy [*sic*] pants, tarpaulin hat, horsehair beard, and buffalo hair mustachios. The Indians know him, and he would stand a poor chance if not disguised.

The place called Burns', which has become noted of late for quartz veins, is an extensive region of rolling land, about six miles on the south side of the Mercede [Merced]. During the rainy season last year some rich diggings were found here. The settlement is now pretty extensive. The people, within the last two or three months, have gathered up an immense quantity of earth, which they cannot wash for want of water. The earth is certain to yield well; but the patience of the traders, who have credited the miners to the extent of their means, is now becoming exhausted. All we want is rain, to cause a revival of business in the south.

As to the quartz veins in the neighborhood of Burns', all is uncertainty as yet. Not less than thirty or forty discoveries of quartz bearing gold have been of late; but much in time and capital may be exponded [*sic*] before the actual value can be ascertained. Doubtless some of them will yield far beyond the expectations of the owners, while others will prove a total failure. One company at Burns' are now putting up expensive machinery, to be worked by steam. These veins are claimed by persons mostly without capital, who are disposed to sell. The locality is certainly worthy of the attention of capitalists.

Yours &c. R. W.

Daily Alta California, February 7, 1851

Savage's Second Expedition—Ten Indians killed and Forty wounded— Murders at Agua Frio and Empire City—The Weather—The Miners— Indian Prophecies—Col. Fremont—The Silver Mountains, &c.

NEAR CASTORIA, Feb. 4, 1851

MESSRS. EDITORS—I have just received an account of Savage's second expedition, which I think you can rely upon. Savage started from Agua Frio with 210 men. On the road Savage started ahead, with seventy men, to reconnoitre [sic], leaving the balance of his force with Maj. Burney. They were to meet at the Fine Gold Gulch. Savage waited one day at that place, but Maj. Burney not coming up he went with his small force in pursuit of the Indians. In the evening he surprised a large force and had a skirmish, the Indians retreating. Next morning, twenty eight of Savage's men took the Indian's trail, came up with them and killed ten and wounded forty. The Indians retreated, and Savage's party returned without effecting anything.

The thirty five men left by Savage, on returning from his first expedition, at Fort Frizne, took forty-eight mules from a party of Indians after Savage left them.

I have just been informed by a gentleman from the Tuolumne, that some friendly Indians who have been camped on that river for some time past, engaged in fishing, having moved their camp to higher ground, and give the whites to understand that they look for much rain shortly. On the other hand, I am informed that Casonse, an Indian chief, predicts a dry winter.

Daily Alta California, January 22, 1853
Marysville

MORE INDIAN DIFFICULTIES—DEATH OF A CHIEF.—A correspondent of the Marysville *Herald*, writing a few weeks since from Lyon's Ranch, gave an account of an affray with the Indians which resulted in the death of eighteen or twenty, writes again under date of 15th inst.

Yesterday evening, information was received that the one chief was at Frenchtown, a mining settlement across the West Branch, four or five miles distant, openly threatened vengeance upon the whites for the severe castigation they had received.

A party of eight was immediately formed, and at 6 o'clock set out from Hasty's Ranch, crossed the river, arrested and brought back the old chief, arriving before 11 o'clock. After binding him, a strong guard was placed over him to prevent the possibility of his escape, until this morning, when he was removed about a mile, to Lyon's Ranch, and after a short deliberation, it was unanimously resolved to hang him at once. Arrangements were soon made and the redoubtable old brave, who had figured so conspicuously in every Indian affray of importance in this region, since the introduction of the whites, after calmly surveying the preparations made for his execution, met his fate with consummate bravery. He was suspended by the neck to the limb of an oak in the neighborhood.

The vote deciding upon this course was unanimous, but there is at least one who strongly doubts the policy or justice of the proceeding. Time will show. There are still two chiefs remaining, and a tribe that can muster at least fighting men, in the immediate neighborhood of a small scattered population of exposed and defenseless whites. What course they, toge [sic] her with their allies, the Tigres and Nimekews, will pursue, remains to be seen.

Daily Alta California, February 4, 1853
Indian Robberies on Dry Creek.—Fights with the Indians

The house of Messrs. Bragg & Drew, situated on the Mckeiumne river, near the junction of Dry Creek, was entered and robbed of a large quantity of goods. Mr. Drew, accompanied by another gentleman, went in search of the robbers, and from well-founded suspicions entertained, visited an Indian rancheria not far off. Here they discovered a lot of goods for which they were in search. They asked the Indians to deliver the goods over, as the property of Messrs. Bragg & Drew, which request they refused to comply with. A chief of the tribe held a pistol over the head of Mr. Drew in a threatening attitude, and told him, "if he didn't leave he would shoot him." Mr. Drew and his companion, not considering it prudent to remain longer, departed.

Information was dispatched throughout the neighborhood of these facts, with a request for an assembling of the whites.

A party of sixteen armed and proceded [sic] to the Indian village, and informed them that they did not come to fight but to reclaim the goods. While thus parlaying one of the Indians was seen to raise his rifle and fired, but missed. This was the signal for an unanimous fire from the whites, killing four of the Indians. The Indians retreated and the whites kept up a continued fire till their ammunition was exhausted when they retired to renew the contest with a reinforcement. In the meantime the Indians had taken refuge on an island in Dry creek, surrounded on all sides by a broad stream of water. Having stolen all of the boats along that stream or set them adrift, the party were unable to approach them. Their position was found to be regularly fortified by the cutting down of brush wood, and piling it up as a breast work of defense. In reply to inquiries addressed to them from the shore, they said it was their chief who had committed the robbery and that it was also in accordance with his commands that they had fired upon the whites. They refused to give him up and said, with true Spartan heroism, that if the whites desired to secure him, "they must come and take him."

In reply to this insolence the whites again fired upon them. The fire was promptly returned, the Indians showing great bravery and venturing to the very water's edge to discharge their pieces. Their bullets rattled about the heads of the whites in every direction, and to protect themselves they were compelled to adopt the shelter of trees, logs, &c. Night closing in, the party retreated, leaving the Indians masters of the field.

Daily Alta California, March 16, 1853

A difficulty took place between Indians and miners in the vicinity of Tehama, growing out of sundry thefts and depredations, peculiar to the savage race. The Americans, goaded beyond endurance, rose in a body and slaughtered some fifteen or twenty belonging to one tribe.

Daily Alta California, March 21, 1853
Sonora Correspondence.
Severe Encounter with the Indians—the New Diggings

Sonora, Feb. 25th, 1853

I wrote you a day or two since that a body of Indians had descended from the mountains, and stolen a number of horses and mules, and that a party was then gone in pursuit of them. I learn to-day that they have returned, having had a severe brush with the Indians, and recovered nothing. This tribe, which is represented to be one of the lowest and most savage, live near the South Fork of the Stanislaus to which place they were followed by the party, consisting of seventeen well armed men. The pursuing party went boldly into the midst of their rancheria, not observing more than three or four Indians, until they found themselves surrounded by some three or four hundred, some armed with guns, some with revolvers, and some with bows and arrows. The Indians at once set upon the party, and they had nothing to do but fight their way through and return, which they did, killing three Indians and wounding several more. None of the Americans were killed or wounded. A large party will probably leave in a few days, for the purpose of giving them a thorough castigation.

Daily Alta California, March 30, 1853

The *Courier* of Saturday contains the following account of a terrible fight with the Pitt River Indians:

Mr. John Nailon arrived in this place on Wednesday, bringing information of a very severe fight between a number of ranchers and the Pitt River Indians on Sugar Loaf Mountain.

He arrived at the Sugar Loaf Mountains, on his return trip from Yreka, Tuesday, in company with a party of ten men and forty mules, where he met Mr. Brener with a party of about twenty men, engaged in severe conflict with the Indians. He represents the mountain literally alive with those red devils, who had selected a position where they had every advantage over the whites, the only indications of their presence being a continual flight of arrows, accompanied by the most terrible yells. Mr. N. and his party—their mules unpacked—fought their way through at once, leaving Brener and his men to make good their way over the mountain. When Mr. N. reached the Back Bone, he heard firing in the direction of Sugar Loaf, and supposed that Brener's party was still engaged with the Indians.

The Indians had fire arms, but did no execution with them, not charging their guns with a sufficient quantity of powder. How many of Brener's party were killed is not known here at this time, no parties having arrived over that trail since the fight.

Mr. Durnad, with a pack train, was met by Mr. N. about ten miles beyond the scene of conflict. He had two of his mules shot the same day, although he succeeded in saving their cargoes.

Sugar Loaf Mountain is about twenty-five miles to the north of this place, immediately in the Sacramento trail leading from Shasta to Yreka.

A meeting was to have been held on the evening of the 26th, to form a company to hunt the Pitt River Indians from the Sacramento trail.

A party of coast range Indians was attacked by two white men for stealing cattle belonging to Mr. Middleton. A desperate fight ensued—the two whites putting the entire band to fight, after killing eight of their number.

On Tuesday the 22nd an Indian was captured and shot through the head for stealing. Another was hung at Reading's ranch for the same crime.

Joaquin and a portion of his band are believed by the *Courier* to be lurking about somewhere in the northern region. On this subject it says—

"Mr. Lusk of Rhodes & Lusk's and Mr. Tracy, of Adam's & Co.'s Express, say that six Mexicans, carrying each twenty-four shots, passed through Colusa a few days since on their way up the Sacramento Valley. The same party, a few days after, when observed by Mr. Morse, of Baxter & Co.'s line of stages, on the road a short distance below this place. Just before leaving Colusa, one of the party, with a scar upon his cheek, and in other respects answering to the description of Joaquin, remarked to some persons present that they might not know him then, but that they would hear from him in a short time."

The *Courier* says that the command under Lieuts. Bates and Ranford, recently sent over the Sacramento trail to Yreka, at last accounts was stopping about twenty-five miles this side Shasta Valley, and about some fifty miles beyond the Sugar Loaf Mountain, the scene of the late Indian fight.

Daily Alta California, June 14, 1853

MORE TROUBLE WITH THE SHASTA INDIANS.—The Shasta *Courier* of Saturday is informed by a correspondent at Jacksonville that much excitement still exists in that vicinity against the Indians. There has been lately, he says, much interest manifested by the citizens of Jacksonville, relative to the white woman supposed to be a prisoner among the Indians. It is believed that she has been detained among them since late 1851. A party of 25 men some days since started out with the intention of recovering her if possible. They arrived at the Indian Camp on Butte Creek, some 40 miles from Jacksonville, and on demanding the woman, were shown an old squaw. The party then removed to the opposite side of the creek, and camped for the night. On the morning following they were visited by eight or ten Indians, who were informed that unless they delivered up the woman at once they would be killed. At this the Indians became frightened, and attempted to make their escape, when six of them were shot down, and the others wounded. The party then returned to Rogue River for provisions. Some fifteen of them have again gone on the search, determined to risk their lives to rescue her from her horrible situation. These are the words of the writer. Whether there was sufficient in the conduct of the Indians who visited the camp to justify the shooting of the six who were slain, judging from this statement, we leave the reader to determine.

Head Quarters
Fort Miller Cal
Feb. 24, 1854
Major E. D. Townsend
Asst. Adjt. General

Dept. of the Pacific
Sir,
I have to report that an inoffensive Indian was barbarously murdered about
12 o'clock last knight by a white man at the rancheria within a few hundred
yards of this post. The act was perpetrated in the most brutal manner by one
of that class of lawless ruffians, whose wanton aggressions upon the Indians
in different parts of this State, have so often provoked retaliation.

The murderer has escaped, but a warrant for his arrest has been issued.

Respectfully,
Yr. Obedt. Servt.
H. W. Wessells
Capt. 2nd Infy, Bvt. Major Comdg.

(National Archives, Records of the War Department, Record Group 98,
Letters Received, Department of Pacific, 1854, Box No. 2, Document W12, as
quoted in *The Destruction of California Indians*, p. 17.)

February, 1859
The Indian War in the North

The expedition against the Northern Indians is over, and a permanent peace
has been established by the capture of the belligerent tribes and their removal
to one of the Reservations.

The war was undertaken at the urgent solicitation of many residents of
Humboldt and Trinity counties, who averred that their property had been
despoiled, and that their lives were in danger. That the lives of many whites
have been taken by these roaming, well-armed and ferocious tribes—for they
were not like our Diggers—and that their presence, in the hostile attitude
they had assumed and were maintaining was a serious drawback to the settlement and prosperity of that entire section. In accordance to this request
the Governor, who is ex-officio Commander in Chief of the State forces,
ordered mustered into the field a company of eighty men to chastise these
Indians, and ordered Gen. Kibee to accompany the expedition for the purpose of supplying it with all needful things and at the cheapest possible rate.
The Governor also said in his orders: "The women and children must be
spared, and there must be no indiscriminate slaughter of the Indians;
humanity demands that no more blood should be shed than is indispensable
to open the trail and render travel upon it secure and uninterrupted in the
future. You will take care that this order is ready to company which may be
mustered into service."

This does credit to both his head and his heart, for it is not to be denied that Indian Wars conducted by State troops have heretofore, been more like cold blooded massacres than anything else. These orders we are informed, were strictly obeyed wherever it was possible to do so, and the report of the Quartermaster and Adjutant-General, Kibee tells us that but 75 to 100 were killed, a large number wounded and 350 taken prisoners. The campaign commenced in the middle of October last, and was ended in the middle of February. The Indians were scattered over an area of fifty miles square, of an almost impenetrable country. They were watched by day and pursued by night. Their haunts were visited; their hiding-place ascertained and nocturnal descents had to be resorted to as the only means of capturing them. Several old Indian hunters were of the party, and traced the aborigines everywhere, no matter how guarded were their trails. In this four months expedition in mid-winter against hostile Indians in their own haunts known only to themselves, who [sic] numbers were as six or seven to one, compared with their pursuers, not one of the troop lost his life, and but seven were found wounded. Of these seven, four have entirely recovered, and three are yet under medical treatment. The cost of the expedition, not including the pay of the troops, amounted to $32,406.93 which compared to all former expeditions of a like nature, is said to be, and we believe it is very little.

Much credit is given in the report to both officers and men in this expedition and it would seem from all the facts before us that this praise is not undeserved. By this action, a large tract of fertile country has been opened up to actual settlers, and the lives and property of those there residing have been protected from future depredations by the Indians. The Governor and Quartermaster General in their reports and dispatches, having spoken well of the troops, we are free to say that from the best information we have on this subject, these two officers are entitled as the directors of the movement, to no less praise than they have bestowed upon others. To conduct such a campaign with such economy and such humanity, is so rare a spectacle among us that those who have inaugurated a new and better era in this respect, should have at least the satisfaction in knowing that their conduct meets approbation somewhere.

(This quotation is taken from *The Other Californians*, pp. 210–11. The newspaper account has not been identified but the report is in W. C. Kibbe, *Report of the Expedition Against the Indians in the Northern Part of the State*, Chas. T. Botts, State Printer, 1860, 10 pp.)

San Francisco Bulletin, August 6, 1859
Progress of the White Crusade Against Indians in the North

The Red Bluff *Beacon* gives some particulars of the success of "subscription party" in clearing Tehama county of its Indians, who are certainly very troublesome and dangerous to the white settlers. Says the *Beacon*:

The news reached us, from a reliable source, on Monday, August 1st, that sometime during last week the party sent out with John Breckenridge, under pay raised by the subscription, met a party of five Indians and one white man, between the headwaters of Butte and Deer creeks, with whom they engaged in a severe running fight, which only lasted a short time, when Mr. B, and his party succeeded in forever silencing, so far as the straggling band is concerned, hostilities. The red men of the party, as well as their palefaced leader, of whom the country is well rid, are now sleeping the sleep of death. As a trophy, or sort of remembrance that there was a man so base as to lead on a band of savages to deeds of butchery and theft, the scalp of the white man was taken and brought away by Mr. Breckenridge.

The day after this encounter, a large rancheria was discovered, and preparations made for surrounding it during the night. This they only partially succeeded in, owing to the smallness of the company, which only numbers about a dozen men. They succeeded, however, about daylight next morning, in killing ten Indians, including one squaw, who threw herself between a white man and one of the bucks just at the moment of firing off the rifle of the former.

This gallant little army is still in the mountains, and were to attack a much larger rancheria, near the head of Deer Creek, on Saturday night last, the result of which engagement has not reached us.

On Sunday afternoon, about an hour before sunset, while the occupants were absent from home, the houses of Mr. Roundtree and Mr. Anderson, some four and a half miles above the Mayhew's Crossing, on Deer Creek, were set on fire by Indians and entirely consumed, as well as their hay stacks, fencing, etc. The smoke and flames soon aroused the neighborhood, but no Indians were to be seen. Owing to the close proximity of these ranches to the foothills, they were enabled to easily escape and secrete themselves. Their tracks were plainly visible next morning, and no doubt remains as to its being Indians who committed the deed.

The inhabitants of the valley along the foothills are all moving in towards the river for protection. Mr. King of Vermont Mills removed his family down to Mr. Mayhew's on Sunday last, and Mr. Sadorus and family have gone down below Mr. Keefer's on Rock creek. Others, we understand, are leaving every day for more secure quarters.

No doubt now remains that the Indians have white accomplices, and that they receive their supplies of arms and ammunition from white agents. The rancheria stormed last week was found to contain flour, sugar, dishes, and nearly all the comforts usually found in the cabins of white people. It is understood that there are some forty or fifty white brutes living on the headquarters of Butte creek with squaws, in a state of concubinage, and that uphold and protect the Indians in all their depredations. These people doubtless encourage the Indians to steal from the citizens of this valley, and perhaps divide with them in the spoils a large number of American horses and cattle that have been taken from our citizens, and it would be well for General Kibbe's company, before the contemplated campaign upon which he is about to enter is over, to make strict inquiry into this matter and if, as we suspect, there are white receivers of the stolen property taken from this valley, from time to time by Indians, to endeavor to have them brought to justice. The man who was shot last week was, we learned, a stranger to the party that killed him. The conclusion is, by those who live in the vicinity, that he was, in all probability, one of the Butte creek squaw men. (As quoted in *The Destruction of California Indians*, pp. 93–94.)

Sacramento Union, November 8, 1859

Letter from Pitt River—The Indian War—A recointer [*sic*] of scenes passed in the present Indian expedition—The capturing 400 prisoners and the destruction of 80 formidable warriors, by a company of men not exceeding 90 in the short space of 75 days, is worthy not only of repetition, but of much commendation. The Indians have been divided—band from band—pursuing each with rapidity and determination, not allowing them to gather acorns nor seeds sufficient for Winter consumption, despoiled them of their fishing grounds, the source from which they derive their staple nourishment and so hemmed them in that when these mountains become enwrapt in their "snowy mantles," and these valleys assume their hoary costume, they must succumb at the advancing step of the white man or fall beneath his greater facility and power.

If the object was to take all the redskins, I fear the plan would fall short of its anticipation—three months more of the most determined assiduity will not rid these mountains of their aboriginal inhabitants. The rough country over which the Indians are scattered is too extensive, the number of men employed to capture them too few, and the facilities afforded inadequate to do so much in so short a time.

To leave the work undone would be a greater evil than not to have commenced it, for as long as small roving bands remain in the mountains the settlers are not safe from the marauding depredations. Not only that, but the Indian is known to be particularly attached to his childhood home, and as long as any of his kindred remain he will, despite the vigilance of Reservation guards, eventually return to his early stamping ground, and, having a greater knowledge of the sympathies of the white race, will be the greater pest than ever.

H. W. S. Nov. 1, 1859
Sulphur Springs, Pitt River.

San Francisco Bulletin, January 21, 1860
Indian troubles in Mendocino

The Indians have again become very troublesome to the settlers of Mendocino county. Mr. White, a resident of Long Valley, informs us that they have become so bad that the settlers have been compelled to organize themselves into a standing army, so to speak, and by taking turns keep their stock and homes under constant guard. For some time previous to this being done, the Indians had killed from ten to fifteen head of stock nightly. One gentleman alone, Mr. Woodman, has lost 100 head of horses, 74 of which were found dead in a canyon not far from his place, and upon the bodies of which the Indians were having a great feast. On the 19th of December, the settlers turned out, and attacking the enemy succeeded in killing 32 and taking two prisoners. The United States troops located in that region are represented to be pursuing, during all these troubles, a "masterly course of inactivity." The aid of the State has therefore been asked, and will we trust be granted. *Petaluma* Journal, 20th January.

San Francisco Bulletin, June 18, 1860
Indian Butcheries in California

The New York *Century* of 12th May has the following observations upon a matter which has been often laid, in all its terrible details, before the readers of the Bulletin:

We have been informed through the papers, of the murderous outrages committed on the aboriginal inhabitants of California by men with white skins. We regret to say that there is no exaggeration in these accounts. On the contrary, on conversing with a number of individuals who, to some extent, witnessed the transactions, we can bring to light no circumstance to palliate or extenuate them in the slightest degree. In the Atlantic and Western States, the Indians have suffered wrongs and cruelties at the hands of the stronger race. But history has no parallel to the recent atrocities perpetrated in California. Even the record of Spanish butcheries in Mexico and Peru has nothing so diabolical.

Humboldt county, in the northern section of the State, has been the scene of a great portion of these outrages. The perpetrators seem to have acted with a deliberate design to exterminate the Indian race. Their butchery was confined to women and children, the men being absent at that time. They were the Digger tribes, known as friendly Indians, the most degraded and defenseless of the race, entirely destitute of the bold and murderous spirit which characterizes other tribes of red men. They were charged with stealing cattle and other property from the whites, and with selling firearms and ammunition to the hostile tribes. The attack was made in the night, when they were collected in their little settlements or villages at some sort of merry-making. The men were known to be absent—they had possibly fled on suspicion of danger. Under these circumstances, bands of white men, armed with hatchets—small bands but sufficiently numerous for the purpose—fell on the women and children, and deliberately slaughtered them, one and all. Simultaneous attacks were made on the different rancherias or encampments. Fire-arms were scarcely used, the work being done with hatchets.

In one of the settlements, an aged and feeble chief collected the women around him, when they were about flying on the approach of the human bloodhounds, assuring them that white men did not kill squaws and that they would be safe. But they all perished together. One of our informants saw twenty-six bodies of women and children collected in one spot by the more humane citizens preparatory to burial. Some of them were infants at the breast, whose skulls had been cleft again and again. The whole number slaughtered in a single night was about two hundred and forty.

We have spoken of the authors of this butchery as men—white men. So they were. We can invent no logic that will segregate them from our own species. Would that it were possible to do so. The whole number engaged was probably not over fifty or sixty. They were the lowest and most brutal of the border population, such as hang on the outskirts of civilization, and possess nothing of humanity but the form and bestial instincts.

Mendocino county, within a few days' travel of San Francisco, has been the theatre of atrocities nearly parallel, under cover of martial authority. Regularly organized bodies of armed men attacked the settlements of friendly Indians charged with stealing cattle, and murdered them in like manner, except that fire-arms were used and not hatchets. In this case, men, as well as women and children, were massacred. To defray the expenses of this heroic work, enormous claims were presented to the Legislature.

A gentleman who has spent much time in Mendocino county, informs us that the intercourse of the whites with the Clear Lake Indians, as they are called, has laid the foundation for the ultimate extermination of the race by disease, in the manner of the Sandwich Islands. Of five or six hundred squaws, from ten years old and upwards, he was assured that not a solitary individual was exempt! Civilized humanity will scarcely believe it possible for human beings to be degraded so far below savages, as are the filthy wretches who infect the frontier settlements, and commit such deeds of rapine and blood as we have here but inadequately described.

California Farmer, March 27, 1861

The Petaluma Journal of April 15, 1857, says that extensive Indian killing has taken place, and still is occurring in the vicinity of Round Valley. Information has been received in Petaluma, through a gentleman just from there, that within the past three weeks, from 300 to 400 bucks, squaws, and children have been killed by the whites. The cause of this wholesale killing, is stated to be the continued depredations by the Indians upon the stock of the settlers, and a resistance to the Reservation officials, in their attempts to collect the Indians upon the Reservation. In one instance a soldier belonging to Lieut. Dillon's command, was mortally wounded by the Indians. It is stated that the women and children are mostly spared by the settlers, and taken to the Reservation; but the "bucks" are more safely disposed of. (As quoted in *They Were Only Diggers*, pp. 47-48.)

California Farmer, March 27, 1861

Slaughter of Indians near Humboldt Bay.—After speaking of the recent massacre of over 200 Indians near Humboldt Bay, by the white settlers, in April 1860, a writer in the Bulletin goes on to say, all of the bucks who formerly lived round Eureka with their families, having ties that bound them to the Bay and the settlements here, have dispersed to the mountains, and are now seeking vengeance as thieves, for their kindred slain. It will cost not less than half a million dollars to dislodge the 300 thieving Indians from the Bald Hills. Men who detest and abhor the thugging system, from circumstances that surround them, are silent. Two or three men who were on one last Grand Jury which sat at Eureka, were thugs. The man mentioned above is the same person who boasted of having killed 60 infants with his own hatchet at the different slaughter grounds. This is the same man who peddled whiskey to the U.S. soldiers, and the Indians, not 18 months ago, and on the same ground that is now annoyed by the thieving savages. The Indians since the recent grand massacre at Eureka, have done damage to him of not less than $1000; in fact, he will be compelled to leave for some other range for his stock. (As quoted in *They Were Only Diggers*, p. 48.)

Marysville Appeal, April 16, 1862

The *Humboldt Times* says that on the 2nd of April, the citizens of Arcata held a meeting to consider the existing relations with the Indians, at which a series of resolutions were adopted, among which were the following: Resolved, that our community has been laid waste entirely; all of the dwellings have been burnt to the east of the Hoopa trail, "except one now occupied by the troops, " for a distance of near 50 miles east and south; the cattle and other property destroyed to a great extent; our citizens have been murdered by the score; the women and little children have been driven to our village and are nearly destitute. For more than one year, citizens have been prevented from going to the country except at the great risk of their lives. Improvement of any kind is now out of the question, and we have been mortified by seeing our population steadily take their departures for other parts of the country, affording more security.

Resolved, that patience with us, with these Indians, and with everything except that which is manly, practical, and fully adequate to the immediate removal of the various tribes from our midst, has ceased to be a virtue, the trials of 12 years, and the gloom by barbarous murders being more than we can bear.

Resolved, that we have a feeling of insecurity because of the exposed position and the defenseless condition of this village.

Resolved, that we request of those in authority to remove the Hoopa tribe of Indians, (by force, if necessary,) who are liable to an outbreak at any moment, some of whom we suppose to be now leagued with those who are depredating upon us, and whose habitation, distant 35 miles only from Arcata, is in the direct path of trade with all the mining region, thereby greatly retarding the prosperity of this community, as well as those depending upon us. (As quoted in *They Were Only Diggers*, p. 87.)

Sacramento Union, November 21, 1865
Horrid Murder of an Indian Boy

The Shasta Courier of November 18th describes a recent tragedy in its county, as follows:

Near North Fork of Cottonwood, week before last, a most cowardly and barbarous murder was committed. It seems that two white barbarians went to an Indian rancheria in that neighborhood for the purpose of getting possession of an Indian girl about ten years old. This attempt at forcible possession was resisted by the mother of the child, assisted by a crippled Indian boy, the only one at the rancheria. The resistance of this poor cripple so exasperated the villains that one of them seized him by the top of the head, while with his knife he first cut his throat and then stabbed him to the knife hilt, and to wreak his vengeance fully, turned the knife in the wound several times, then withdrawing it, again stabbed his victim, turning the knife as before, repeating the act until life was extinct. While this butchery was going on, the girl and her mother made their escape. In a few days after, the fiends burnt the rancheria. There is nothing but the dead body and Indian testimony to prove the above, and though it is convincing, it is not enough, under the law, to punish the miscreants. White men who live with Indians habitually should do so subject to Indian testimony; and we think a law to that effect would be wise and proper.

Yreka Semi-Weekly Union, February 6, 1864
Orleans Bar, Jan. 28, 1864

ED. UNION:—The hostile Indians have commenced in earnest their warfare of butchering and massacre in Klamath County. I suppose you already have published the assassination of the victims of the South Fork of Salmon—League, Yesters, Roberts, Starkup, Bedwin, and Italian Frank. The murder of these men may be fully attributed to the amount of "red tape" surrounding the service of our citizens who volunteered in the "service" with the express understanding that they were to be actively engaged in fighting Indians and NOTHING ELSE. Had the volunteers in the Indian service been tolerably managed, it is the conviction of all of our citizens that the hostile Indians would long since have been terminated, but alas, circumlocution and red tape has so bound up the usefulness of our Indian fighting volunteers, that the red devils who infest the counties of Klamath, Humboldt, and Trinity have only been emboldened, and with them the name of a soldier is a by-word and a jeer.

I do not know who is to blame, of my own knowledge, in the management of the companies raised to fight Indians and give security to the inhabitants of this region, and can only echo the universal and general sentiment and opinions I hear expressed by others in this section. The blame is laid upon Col. Whipple; I have never heard during the last four or five months expressed but one opinion in reference to his ability, and action, as the commanding officer of these companies, and that unfavorable. Certainly, the result of his do-nothing policy has proven very disastrous to life and property in Klamath county; on the other hand Major Taylor is generally liked and it is believed that if left to his own discretion he would change the order of things and rid us of all hostile Indians.

There is "A rottenness in Denmark" somewhere, in the management of our Indian affairs, and the citizens are now forming INDEPENDENT companies to follow the Indians into their mountain fastnesses and annihilate them. A company of twenty-odd white men, together with about thirty friendly fighting Klamath Indians, under the command of Sheriff F. M. Brown, will leave here in a day or two in search of the notorious "Jim" and his band of cut throats; they will be prepared to remain out a month or two. Two small companies, I understand, are, also, organized in the upper end of the county for the same object.

It is a burning shame that a couple of hundred of brute Diggers cannot be subdued by the REGULAR forces raised for that express purpose, but it is nevertheless true, and the citizens are now compelled to leave their usual avocations, and do up the business they have already most liberally contributed men and means to accomplish. (As quoted in *They were only Diggers*, pp. 90–91.)

Chapter 6

★ ★

INDIAN RELATIONS WITH THE STATE AND FEDERAL GOVERNMENTS

The Gold Rush attracted tens of thousands of American citizens to California. With the signing of the Treaty of Guadalupe Hidalgo, California formally fell under the jurisdiction of the United States. California soon became a state under the Compromise of 1850. The new state government, dominated by whites, quickly passed a statute that specifically discriminated against Native Americans and sought to place them in a subservient position within Anglo society. This law, known as "An Act for the Government and Protection of Indians," is reprinted in this section. Like the Jim Crow laws of the South, these laws sought to discriminate, but California's laws targeted Native Americans, not African Americans.

In addition to this legalized bigotry and assumption of federal power in Indian relations, the state of California set aside $1.5 million to reimburse volunteer militia units that hunted down and killed so-called hostile Indians. Thus, the state of California paid men to murder Native Californians. One of these vigilante groups—the Mariposa Battalion—tormented and disrupted indigenous societies in a region known as the Southern Mines. These ruffians sought to murder as many Native Americans as possible and then coerce survivors to sign treaties with federal agents.

As some of the following documents demonstrate, the federal government dispatched three commissioners—Redick McKee, George Barbour, and O. M. Wozencraft—to negotiate agreements with the indigenous inhabitants of California. They negotiated eighteen treaties with California's tribes, which the United States Senate rejected. At one time, California's tribes controlled all of the land, water, minerals, and other resources of the region, but under the treaties of the 1850s, they would have lost most of their estate. However, they would have retained for themselves approximately one-seventh of the state as

Indian reservations. Even this was too much for whites in California, and the California delegation worked feverishly to scuttle the treaties so that the native people had little formal relationship with the federal government, so that the state could assert its powers over the Indians. As a result, California allowed whites to steal Indian land, enslave Indian children, rape native women, and murder indiscriminately Indian men, women, and children.

In 1852, Edward Beale was appointed the superintendent of Indian Affairs in California. He subsequently established the first official Indian reserves within the Golden State. In spite of reservations, Native Californians lost their land, resources, and children. They lost their lives and health. However, despite these methods to subjugate indigenous peoples, Native Americans continued to resist Anglo assaults. Indians also carried out numerous raids on American communities. For instance, one letter addressed to California governor John Bigler mentions that Native Americans recently killed at least 110 whites and either seized or destroyed $240,000 worth of property in four counties. Such documents—questionable at best—encouraged increased hostilities against native societies. Government appropriations and the formation of militia units undoubtedly resulted from this information. All in all, the state government of California and the United States federal government ardently strived to destroy the traditional ways of life of California's first nation's people.

Daily Alta California, January 1, 1851
Indian Difficulties

Every little while war panics break out in new places. The great El Dorado Indian war bubble has scarcely burst ere another terrific cry is raised through one of the Stockton papers and echoed here, in which one would be left to suppose that a perfect annihilating war has broken out among the poor starving Indians of the southern mines. Now, if we subtract one half of the whole as the exaggeration of rumor, and at least one half of the other half in consideration of the medium through which it is published, and then attribute all that is left to the uncalled for oppressions of the unprincipled who are found among the white population, we shall have the whole matter in a fair estimate. It is said that the Indians have all gone into the mountains resolved to exterminate the whites, and that they are in force to the amount of five or six thousand. They have been abused and may have retired from the presence of whites, but that they are so strong or so determined we doubt entirely.

In this state of affairs some are calling lustily upon the state government to put an end to the misunderstanding. They had better call upon the shade of Daniel Boone, or some straw representation of a state government. Has our government done anything yet for the prosperity and peace of California? Nothing. We are not aware that it is this day any better off from the effects of any acts of the state cabinet, than it would have been without any. The state government has nothing in its purse, and we fear as little in its brains for helping the public out of, or keeping it out of difficulties. We have seen nothing yet that showed activity, or energy, or ability, in the management of state affairs. The Indians have as little respect for and confidence in the powers that have had a nominal rule in California, as have the white population, and it would only be embroiling still worse if the two races for a straw government to interfere.

Happily we have now among us two gentlemen, appointed by the government at Washington, to settle all difficulties with the Indian tribes, and they will, in conjunction with the third, Maj. Barbour, when he shall have arrived—being expected by the next steamer—represent the U.S. Government to these poor despised children of the forests and mountains, and protect them. The U.S. Courts will soon be organized throughout our State, and then we hope to see every man who commits an outrage upon the poor Indian, hauled up before them, and have justice dealt out to him, without any mock pity or commiseration. As it is, a few low unprincipled villains outrage all the feeling of humanity and decency in their intercourse with the Indians until they can endure it no longer, and then the innocent are generally the sufferers. Nearly all the difficulties with Indians in this country have originated in outrages upon them by the unhung rascals who disgrace our nation and our race. Our Indian Commissioners and Agents, we hope, will effect a happy change in these things.

Daily Alta California, January 13, 1851

The Select Committee appointed by the Assembly upon the subject of Claims against the General Government, reported a preamble and resolutions introducing our representatives in Congress to use their best efforts to procure the passage of a law providing for the payment to California of the monies [sic] expended by her in the suppression of Indian disturbances. The report was laid upon the table.

Daily Alta California, January 14, 1851

Below we publish an address of the Agents appointed by the General Government for the purpose of treating with the Indians, to the people of

California. We commend it to the attention of those living in the Indian Districts, and trust that it will be respected. The agents proceed this day to the capital at San José.

To the People of California, residing in the vicinity of the Indian Troubles: The undersigned, appointed by the President of the United States, Special Commissioners, with plenary powers to visit and negotiate treaties of peace and friendship, with the various tribes of Indians in California, deem it proper in this way, to announce their arrival in the country, and their intention to enter upon the important duties of their mission, as early as the state of the weather, and of the roads, will admit of travelling. In the meantime, hearing of the difficulties which have recently existed, and are said to still exist, on the borders of the Sacrament and San Joaquin rivers, as well as in other parts of the State, the Commissioners appeal to their fellow citizens, in such disturbed districts to adopt and pursue toward the Indians a course of conduct marked by mildness, moderation and forbearance—holding themselves wholly on the *defensive*, at least until time shall be afforded us to investigate, and, if practicable, redress their grievances.

All good citizens and emigrants are interested in restoring to the frontier settlements the peaceful and amiable relations which once so happily existed between them and the Indians.

That in some of the difficulties which have recently occurred the Indians have been the aggressors—that the whites have had much provocation to justify the severity of their measures of retaliation, will not be denied; still, so far as our information extends, many lives have been sacrificed, and much ill feeling engered [*sic*] unnecessarily.

The Indians of this country are represented as extremely ignorant, lazy and degraded, at the same time generally harmless and peaceable in their habits, indisposed to controversy, or, war with the whites, until goaded to seek revenge for injuries inflicted upon them. For them many allowances should be made. Their very imbecility, poverty, and degradation, should, with enlightened and liberal white men, entitle them to commiseration and long forbearance.

They were the original owners and occupants of those beautiful valleys and mountain ranges, Their fishing and hunting grounds, and acorn orchards, surrounding the graves of their father for many generations, were long unclaimed by other. Until the discovery of the golden treasures, contained in the mountain gorges and water courses of California, the white and red man lived together in peace and mutual security. Since that period, we are informed, the Indian has been by many considered and treated as an intruder, as a common enemy of the whites, and in many instances shot down with as little compunction as a deer or an antelope.

As there is now *no further west* to which they *can* be removed, the General Government and the people of California appear to have left but one alternative in relation to these remnants of once numerous and powerful tribes. viz: *extermination* or *domestication*. As the latter includes all proper measures for their protection and gradual improvement, and secures to the people of the State an element greatly needed in the development of its resources, viz: cheap labor—it is the one which we deem the part of wisdom to adopt, and, if possible, consummate.

It will be our earnest endeavor to quiet the difficulties which now exist, and afford to both whites and Indians, throughout California such protection of property as their good conduct may entitle them to.

It is essential to the character of the State, and indeed of the United States, as a civilized and Christian nation, that a stop should be put to the shedding of blood. If hereafter depredations are committed by the Indians, upon either the person or property of the whites, and you will apprize [*sic*] us of the facts, we will use all proper exertion to bring the offenders to justice, by the military force of the united States, or otherwise.

If, on the other hand, an Indian, or Indians shall be killed in your neighborhood by a white man or a body of white men, without the authority of the law, we request that in like manner, information may be sent to us. The shooting in cold blood, of a white man by an Indian, is *murder* punishable by *death*. So likewise if an Indian be killed by a white man, the crime is the same, the punishment should be the same, and the safety and security of every community demands that equal and exact justice be meted out to all alike. We design paying our respects to your Governor and other public functionaries at San José, and hope to obtain from them much valuable information touching our proposed duties. Ere long we shall hope to meet many of you in your respective neighborhoods, and avail ourselves of your experience and advice in effecting the objects in view.

Very Respectfully, Your Obd't Serv'ts.
REDICK McKEE
GEO. W. BARBOUR
O. M. WOZENCRAFT
San Francisco, Jan. 13, 1851.

P.S. So far as opportunities may serve the Commissioners will feel obliged if intelligent miners, traders, &tc., will take pains to explain the purport of this paper to the chiefs and head men of such tribes as they may meet.

Compiled Laws of California

Chapter CL.

AN ACT for the Government and Protection of Indians. [Passed April 22, 1850.]

The People of the State of California, represented in Senate and Assembly, do enact as follows:

SECTION 1. Justices of the peace shall have jurisdiction in all cases of complaints by, for, or against Indians, in their respective townships in this state.

SEC. 2. Persons and proprietors of lands on which Indians are residing shall permit such Indians peaceably to reside on such lands, unmolested in the pursuit of their usual avocations for the maintenance of themselves and families: Provided, the white person or proprietor in possession of such lands may apply to a justice of the peace in the township where the Indians reside, to set off such Indians a certain amount of land for the necessary wants of such Indians, including the site of their village or residence, if they so prefer it; and in no case shall such selection be made to the prejudice of such Indians, nor shall they be forced to abandon their homes or villages where they have resided for a number of years; and either party feeling themselves aggrieved, can appeal to the county court from the decision of the justice: and then divided, a record shall be made of the lands so set off in the court so dividing them, and the Indians shall be permitted to remain thereon until otherwise provided for.

SEC. 3 Any person having or hereafter obtaining a minor Indian male or female, from the parents or relations of such Indian minor, and wishing to keep it, such person shall go before a justice of the peace in his township, with the parents or friends of the child, and if the justice of the peace becomes satisfied that no compulsory means have been used to obtain the child from its parents or friends, shall enter on record, in a book kept for that purpose, the sex and probable age of the child, and shall give to such person a certificate, authorizing him or her to have the care, custody, control and earnings of such minor, until he or she attain the age of majority. Every male Indian shall be deemed to have attained his majority at eighteen and the female at fifteen years.

SEC. 4. Any person having a minor Indian in his care, as described in the foregoing section of this act, who shall neglect to clothe and suitably feed such minor Indian, or shall inhumanly treat him or her, on conviction thereof shall be subject to a fine not less than ten dollars, at the discretion of a court or jury; and the justice of the peace, in his discretion, may place the minor Indian in the care of some other person, giving him the same rights and liabilities that the former master of said minor was entitled and subject to.

SEC. 5. Any person wishing to hire an Indian, shall go before a justice of the peace with the Indian, and make such contract as the justice may approve, and the justice shall file such contract in writing in his office, and all the contracts so made shall be binding between the parties; but no contract between a white man and an Indian, for labor shall otherwise be obligatory on the part of an Indian.

SEC. 6. Complaints may be made before a justice of the peace, by white persons or Indians; but in no case shall a white man be convicted of any offence [sic] upon the testimony of an Indian, or Indians. And in all cases it shall be discretionary with the court or jury after hearing the complaint of an Indian.

SEC. 7. If any person forcibly conveys any Indian from his home, or compels him to work, or perform any service against his will, in this state, except as provided in this act, he or they shall, on conviction, be fined in any sum not less than fifty dollars, at the discretion of the court or jury.

SEC. 8. It shall be the duty of the justices of the peace, once in six months in every year, to make a full and correct statement to the court of sessions of their county, of all moneys received for fines imposed on Indians, and all fees allowed for services rendered under the provisions of this act; and said justices shall pay over to the county treasurers of their respective counties, all money they may have received for fines and not appropriated, or fees for services rendered under this act; and the treasurer shall keep a correct statement of all money so received, which shall be termed the "Indian fund' of the county. The treasurer shall pay out any money of said funds in his hands, on a certificate of a justice of the peace of his county, for fees and expenditures incurred in carrying out the provisions of this law.

Daily Alta California, January 16, 1851

TROOPS FOR THE INDIANS.—We understand that Col. Adam Johnson, the Indian Agent, yesterday proceeded to Sonoma for the purpose of inducing Gen. Smith to send out some of the U.S. troops to protect the inhabitants of the Mariposa region from the incursions of fighting the whites to the death. We were told that he had received information that a band of about a hundred chiefs and warriors had assembled and avowed their intention of fighting the whites to the death. We have heard nothing more of the contents of the express than the information contained in the letter of our San José correspondent of the 11th instant.

Daily Alta California, January 22, 1851

Our San Jose Correspondence.—The letter of our correspondence "J." treats of very important matters, especially in reference to the Indian hostilities. Those troubles arose at a fortunate time for the Legislature; it could not have managed to "raise the wind" for the current progress of the ship of state. We refer the reader to this interesting letter.

Daily Alta California, January 22, 1851
SAN JOSE INTELLIGENCE
Special Correspondence

San Jose, Jan. 20, 1851

The recent alarming intelligence from Mariposa County has persuaded Gov. McDougall that military operations against the Indians must be conducted on a more liberal scale than he originally contemplated. This intelligence has decided him to take steps for the organization and concentration, at Agua Frio, of a military force which will put a termination to hostilities at one blow. The intimation contained in my letter of yesterday was correct, and the Governor will, to-morrow morning, send in a special message to the Legislature. It is presumed that a simple official communication to the Legislature of the intelligence received from the Indian quarter will be all that is necessary to ensure their prompt and vigorous cooperation with Gov. McDougall in the measures which the emergency demands.

Daily Alta California, January 24, 1851
The Indian Commissioners

We happen to know something about the commission, something of its members, something of its intentions. Of the commission we can tell the Legislature and Gov. McDougall, what they already probably know that is has ample powers to treat, and form treaties, with the Indians, that they have a *carte blanc* [sic] for that purpose, that they are prepared with proper goods for presents, and can draw upon the U.S. officers here for such funds as are necessary. In reference to the members of that commission we may say that we have a full confidence in their ability and integrity to consummate their mission in a manner honorable to their government, advantageous to our citizens, and for the best future of the Indians.

As to their intentions and movements. Their intentions are peaceable treaties and extinguishment [sic] of Indian titles, if it can be peacefully effected. For this relinquishment of course they are empowered to secure to the native occupants of the soil a remunerative consideration in the way of installments or some other equally satisfactory and protective, which shall amply pay the Indians for the rights which they yield, and secure to them the means of subsistence. The article in the *News* of Wednesday, and referred to by Mr. McCorkle, as reported by the *San Jose Argus,* "that Dr. Wozencraft had gone to Sonoma for U.S. troops, to proceed against these Indians" is not correct. We saw and conversed with Dr. Wozencraft yesterday, and know that such is not the case.

When the Commissioners first arrived, Gen. Smith offered to place at their disposal such force as they thought necessary, if he had that force at command. He at the same time suggested, what they had already determined upon, viz: that they would not approach the Indians in a hostile manner, but first exhaust all peaceable means to effect the object of their mission. To approach them with a powerful force of troops would only defeat their purpose. Dr. Wozencraft has been to Benicia, not to Sonoma, and has only made a requisition upon Gen. Smith for an escort.

Gen. S. has, however, determined to call together all the U.S. forces suitable for a campaign against the Indians, should that course unhappily become necessary. Those stationed in Oregon, as well as at different points in this State, will, we have been assured, be concentrated so that they may at once be put into active service in suppressing the hostilities if peaceable measures fail. That the Indians may have to be punished severely and made to feel our power ere they will listen to wisdom and act in good faith, is quite probable; but at any rate, peace measures will first be tried. This is right; therefore we do not regret the moderate manner with which our Legislature seems determined to act respecting these disturbances, In the first place, everything which is reported about them is a huge exaggeration, much of it rumor, much colored by individual desire for speculation, and much downright lying by those who are anxious for peculation by means of an Indian war, or any other way.

Mr. Baldwin has the right of the matter. The law is sufficient now, without special enactment to authorise [sic] the sheriff of the counties to call out sufficient force to protect the inhabitants from depredations, and the miners of those counties are the men best capable of performing the service. It would be a piece of unworthy meddling, should our State government throw any insuperable barrier between our Commissioners and the pacification of the tribes. A force of volunteers would be certain to do that; and, besides, it seems that these hostilities are seized upon as a pretext for issuing $300,000 State scrip, with an avidity which shows plainly that the object is not so much, on the part of some, a defence [sic] of the miners as a fleeing of the people.

We deny emphatically the right of the Legislature to pass any such act upon grounds partaking so much of *rumor,* and so very uncertain in all respects as to facts. We say again that there are persons who would willingly plunge the country in war, and the State into a million dollars of indebtedness, could they thereby make a fortune. This whole matter belongs to the United States Government. She has troops enough and money enough on this coast to make the war, carry it on, and pay its expenses. She has as fine a set of officers here as can be produced any where, and a little skirmishing would be to them pastime. Let the State authorities, therefore, attend to their own legitimate business, plunge the State no further in debt, and leave to Uncle Sam and his servants to conduct this matter, which belongs exclusively to them.

Daily Alta California, January 24, 1851
Special Correspondence

SAN JOSE, Jan. 22, 1851

An appropriation of the public moneys for any purpose whatever, no matter how necessary, is an act which is always contemplated with horror and indignation by several members of the Assembly. It is usually resisted as an arbitrary and unconstitutional usurpation of power which no necessity or danger can justify. Whether these gentlemen are anxious to be known as economists, or whether they are political monomoniacs [*sic*] cannot at present be determined. At the beginning of the session I had occasion to call your attention to the fact that a motion to print the Standing Rules of the House was resisted upon similar grounds. Members having upon that occasion declared that they would resign their seats unless they were furnished with copies of the rules, the economists finally permitted them to be printed.

I have now to notice the fact that the bill which passed the Senate last night, authorizing Governor to empower the Sheriff of Mariposa county to call out a volunteer force of only 250 men, for the purpose of protecting the citizens of that county from the merciless tomahawk and scalping knife of the Indians, was defeated in the House to-day, because it appropriated the pittance of $10 per diem for the pay of each volunteer. The appeal which the Executive has made upon the Legislature for aid in this alarming exigency has therefore been denied by the economists because the war cannot be carried on without an expenditure of money!

The following are the ayes and noes upon a motion to postpone the bill indefinitely:

Ayes-Messrs. Baldwin, Bennett, Bodley, Bradford, Brown, Campbell, Carr, Carnes, Kellogg, McCandless, McCorkle, McDugal, Moore, Pico, Robinson, Saunders, Staerns-17.

Noes-Messrs. Crane, Field, Hall, Hoff, Kendrick, Lisle, Merritt, Murphy, Richardson, Thorne, Wethered, Wilkins, Yeiser, Speaker-14.

So the bill was indefinitely postponed, and the people of Mariposa must take care of themselves, if they can. While the bill was before the Senate, last evening, Gov. McDougal was present, manifesting the utmost interests in its fate, and, by his presence, aiding and encouraging its passage. I am at a loss to account for the vote given by his brother in favor of the indefinite postponement of the bill.

While upon this subject, I wish to state that it is not true, as stated by the *Argus* of this morning, that Dr. Wozencraft, one of the U.S. Commissioners, has gone to Sonoma to procure a detachment of U.S. troops, with a view to lead them against the Indians. It is, however, true that he is on a visit to Gen. Smith's headquarters at Sonoma, to procure an escort for himself and the other Commissioners.

The Finance Committee of the Senate have not yet reported the bill which they were directed to report by a resolution of the Senate, authorizing a "war loan" of $300,000.

Daily Alta California, February 12, 1851
The Indian Expedition

STOCKTON, Sunday, Feb. 9, 1851

The Indian expedition is now making active preparations for a move to the Mariposa. The members of the commission, as you know, left your city on Friday afternoon last, for this place, upon the steamboat Capt. Sutter, and remained at Benicia all night. In the morning, the military escort, under command of Capt. E. D. Keyes, 3d Artillery, composed of companies F and M, of 31st, and Capt. Moore, and McClean of the Infantry, and Gibson and Lendrum of the Artillery—Capt. E. K. Kane, quarter master of the expedition. The troops arrived in good order in the Sutter and Santa Clara, this morning, were immediately disembarked, and are now encamped near the steamboat landing. The Quarter Master and Commissary are making every exertion to facilitate the speedy departure of the expedition; but I do not think it will get off for a couple of days.

It will prove of interest and the readers of the *Alta* shall receive all information concerning its progress and results, every opportunity, my intention being to accompany it, as you are aware.

There is no news of interest stirring here. A new and very elegant little theatre has just been completed, and will open Monday night with a portion of the Jenny Lind theatrical company.

The presence of the troops to-day, with the *attaches* of the commission, has created some little stir in town during the day, and rendered its appearance quite lively. Nothing else of interest.

J. E. D.

P.S.—Col. J. Neely Johnson arrived to-day from San José, and intends leaving tomorrow for Dent's Crossing, on the Stanislaus river, accompanied by Judge Marvin. There is now a company at that place of about 100 strong, and authority has been offered by the State to raise double the amount of rangers, if necessary. I cannot ascertain what the course of proceedings will be, but imagine it will only be employed in case of an outbreak, as they would certainly not jeopardise [*sic*] the course intended by the commissioners. *Nous verrons.*

Daily Alta California, February 15, 1851
Synopsis of Events

Since the departure of the last steamer for Panama the Indian difficulties have been on the increase rather than otherwise, and murders, robberies, and reports of hostilities, collisions and battles have been rife. Efforts have been made in Legislature to raise funds and State troops for carrying on the war. One of the Governor's aids, J. Neely Johnson, Esq., has been despatched by his Excellency to the scene of disturbances, to act on the part of the State with the U.S. Indian Commissioners. Authority has been given to raise a force of volunteers, to be used in case of necessity. The Commissioners have also left Stockton with an escort of some hundred U.S. troops, and it is confidently believed that if no obstacles are thrown in their way by revengeful or interested men, they will be able to form treaties with the mountain tribes and thus give quiet to the country. They are men of the right stamp, acquainted with the Indian character, and disposed to deal justly with them, we believe.

Daily Alta California, February 20, 1851
Camp on San Joaquin, Near Graysonville
Sunday, Feb. 15th, 1851

Last evening about 9 o'clock, Dr. Wozencraft and Col. Barbour, of the Indian Commission, came into camp, accompanied by twelve Indians, under command of *El Capitan* Don Manuel. They are friendly Indians, formerly belonging to the Mission of Santa Clara—as slovenly, lazy, degraded and miserable looking as those we see in our streets daily. The redoubtable *Capitan* is of smaller stature, and dresses in a scarlet jacket, with wings upon the shoulders. Its appearance denotes that it was made for some cavalry officer in the Spanish service, in or about the year 1824. They were furnished with rations for three days, and soon retired to the comforts of their *serapes*, after gobbling up the Commissary's issue.

I learned from Dr. Wozencraft that after leaving Stockton, on Tuesday, his party proceeded to Dent's Crossing on the Stanislaus river, where they summoned the heads of two tribes in that vicinity, to a "talk." The Commissioner's invitation was accepted by José Jesus and Packano, both of them friendly Indians. They expressed their readiness to cultivate the lands and live upon terms of the most amicable intercourse with the whites, preferring that mode of livelihood to larceny. They were unwilling to go out among the hostile tribes to endeavor them to induce them to come in and hold a parley. The Commissioners then proceeded to Cornelius' Ferry, about 35 miles from the mouth of the Tuolomne, near Hawe's Ferry. Old Cornelius, one of the "friendlys," [*sic*] has a rancho there, and has, it is said, much influence over the Indian tribes. Cypriano, the chief of another tribe, against who [*sic*] much suspicion has existed, was at the rancho. He has been suspected of stealing horses and cattle by the whites, and has recently been suspected of treachery by the hostile Indians, among who [*sic*] he has been living with his tribe for some time past, for which reason he has come down nearer the settlements for safety and for succor. Through the influence of Old Cornelius, Cypriano agreed to take up a number of his men, and bring in the chief of various hostile tribes to the rancho within nine days. The Commissioners and their escort will be at that place ready to receive them.

This morning a dress parade took place in the plain adjacent to the camp, for the edification of the Indians, or to give them an idea of the prowess and strength of our arms. After the parade it was announced that Don Manuel expressed himself highly gratified at the proficiency of the troops, a compliment which the officers doubtless appreciated from the acknowledged science of that accomplished warrior and veteran soldier. One of the officers ironically apologized for not having had an opportunity to shave before the parade took place. I must confess that I consider it somewhat impolite to pay too much court and attention to Indians of the class to which those now in camp belong.

Judge Marvin and Col. Johnson have gone to the Mariposa. It is the intention of the State authorities to station volunteer companies along that river in case of an outbreak. We had a rumor here yesterday that Savage had gone out again after the Indians, but I know not whether it is to be relied upon.

This morning, after parade, the men were all assembled, and religious services were performed. The weather is very fine, the days delightful, the night clear, bright and cold.

A grand mustang chase came off to-day, a number of those in this vicinity uniting to give them a hunt. Upon these vast plain are immense droves of these wild horses, and they are frequently hunted down for the purpose of corralling or lassoing some of their number. The chase was extremely spirited, and would have pleased many of us better had our *cavallos* been in a condition to enable us to participate in the enjoyment of the scene.

Since my acquaintance with the members of the commission I have had an opportunity of forming some estimate of their talents and capabilities to carry out their mission to a successful termination, and I am impressed with the belief that they will be able to do so. Col. McKee is a self-taught man, possessing a great deal of knowledge and information, which he has acquired by remitting assiduity. He is urbane and kind-hearted, and appears desirous of doing everything in his power to make all about him comfortable and happy. Dr. Wozencraft is a man of talent and energy—emphatically a working man. He has been popular in this country from his first advent, and the people of this region appear well pleased that the gentlemen whom they selected to represent them in the formation of the state constitution should have received an appointment of honor and trust from the Untied States Government. Of Col. Barbour I can form no opinion, having seen but little of him. He seems to be a man of energy and sense, somewhat modest and retiring, saying but little. He is highly spoken of by those who know him best. When the expedition moves from this point I shall write again, till when adieu.

J.E.D.

Daily Alta California, February 22, 1851
Casteria Correspondence
The Indian Commissioner.—The Weather.—The Miners.—The Farmers.— Irrigation.—Windmills.—The San Joaquin and San Jose Valleys.—Public Land.

Near Castoria, Feb. 16, 1851

Messrs. Editors:—The escort to the Commissioners appointed to treat with the Indians, under the command of Capt. E. D. Keyes, 3d Artillery, passed this place on Thursday last, on their way to the scene of the late Indian disturbances. On Wednesday I had the pleasure of a visit from Maj. J. E.

Durivage and Lieut. Thomas Roach, of the San Francisco Guards, who accompany the expedition.

Daily Alta California, February 28, 1851
[Editorial Correspondence]
Indian Expedition

CAMP WINN, on the Tuolumne River.
Friday, Feb. 21, 1851

I will avail myself of an express which is to start at noon to-day for Graysonville to dispatch you a few lines touching the progress of this expedition. We are now encamped on the Tuolumne River, a few miles above Hawes' ferry [sic] and Cornelius' rancho, some 35 miles from the mouth of the river, in a fine fertile bottom. It is the site of one of the innumerable towns or cities which have sprung into existence in California during the past year, and has been christened Aspinwall. The title to the land is involved in the law; several parties claiming it. It possesses considerable agricultural advantages, and may be a city "one of these fine days," when you and I are under the sod. Our camp has been named after the fair daughter of one of our State Brigadiers, by an admirer of the fair *demoiselle*, who is "one of us."

We left our camp on the San Joaquin on the afternoon of the 18th, John Indian's party having departed in the forenoon, covered with red shirts and blankets, and filled with *carne* and hard bread, the bounty of Uncle Sam's Commissioners and Commisary [sic]. After crossing the ferry at Graysonville we came but about a mile and camped upon the other side of the San Joaquin, in order to have a fair start in the morning. A small train of pack mules arrived from Stockton during the afternoon, and in the evening Mr. Cummings, on of the *attaches* of the Commission, came into camp, bringing some late papers from San Francisco.

On the 19th we made a march of 16 miles, encamping on the banks of the Tuolumne River at Empire City. This is the most beautifully situated, but as yet, is in its infancy. It boasts of a store, a *fonda* and a hotel, with two or three other buildings. There is not a female in the place. The river is now very low and fordable at the city. Yesterday morning the clouds portended rain, and having fifteen miles before us, but a very inconsiderable number of spires of grass were permitted to grow under our heels *en route*, so that we were at our present locality by a little after one o'clock. It soon after commenced raining smartly, but as soon as the wagons arrived tents were pitched, ditches dug, pots and kettles brought out, fires built and all were intent on ministering to the inner man. About half way from Empire City we were met by a half of a dozen horsemen, who were no less distinguished personages than Major Savage and staff. They had come from Mariposa to meet and confer with the Commissioners respecting the Indian difficulties. The State battalion, mustering one hundred and one, rank and file, was organized a few days since at Agua Frio, near Mariposa, by the election of Savage as a Major. Burney was recommended for the office but declined running, I am told. Savage was elected for his knowledge of the Indians, their language, haunts, etc. While engaged in the organization some of the Indian thieves made a descent and very quietly abstracted about a dozen animals. The command is mostly on foot, there being, I think, not more than twenty animals belonging to it. It is said that there are very few animals in that region, nearly all of them having been stolen by the Indians. As we approach nearer the scene of the recent disturbances, the great "Indian fights" grow "small by degrees and beautifully less," and in all the skirmishes that have taken place the Indians appear to have had rather the beat of it. The numbers of savages have unquestionably been overrated. Major Savage says that he cannot now form a correct estimate of their numbers, although a year ago he possessed statistics which enabled him to come very near the mark. He thinks that at the time there were between Mercedes and Four Creeks, about 18,000 all told out of which there were perhaps 8,000 warrior, of which number there were probably 2,000 *braves*. Since that period, there has been much sickness among them and a very heavy mortality, which has of course materially reduced their numerical strength. He expresses his opinion that the runners of Cypriano will be enabled to bring in the chiefs of a number of the hostile tribes in the early part of the next week, and that they will make a treaty; but from his knowledge of their character he does not anticipate that they will adhere to it. As regards the strength of the force now accompanying the Commissioners, he has stated that it is fully competent to whip all force the Indians can muster, if they can be got at, but he does not anticipate that they will be able to encounter them. Whatever is done must be done quickly—if they will not treat promptly they must be punished at once, before the snow melts and they have an opportunity of slipping over the mountains. The State troops are to be stationed at three different posts, one company of the San Joaquin, one on the head waters of the Trigneau, and one at Mariposa, until further orders. Col. J. N. Johnson, *aide du camp* [sic] to Gov. McDougal, has gone to San José—for what purpose is not known. It is presumed, however, to be for authority to mount the State battalion. I trust if this is the measure desired it will not be carried out. If the Indians are to be pursued in the mountain regions animals will be of but little aid, and they will be constantly stolen by the Indians with the utmost watchfulness on the part of the soldiers. The expense of procuring a sufficient number of animals will be enormous, at least $50,000 at the rates they are at present held at. The cost of maintaining the battalion will be very great, and for my part I believe it be an unnecessary move. There are troops enough of the regular army to afford ample protection and to punish the Indians if necessary, without a regularly organized State force being called into requisition. From all the information I have been able to gather from various sources I cannot conceive that there is any danger of the diggings being broken up and the miners driven off by the incursions of the savages. Indians will steal animals if they have a chance, and if they are left exposed by their owners they are to blame. The miners ought to be able to guard against their thieving operations and prevent them. The boast of the aborigines that they will kill all the whites and drive them from their lands, does not carry so much terror to the one, and is not so much to be dreaded as many people strive to make out. They are certainly the most contemptible and insignificant foe the American people ever had to deal with. One good castigation, a few rounds of buck and ball cartridges from government muskets would make them as docile as so many mountain sheep. They are not well armed—their bows and arrows are only serviceable at short distances, and what few rifles and "six shooters" they have are of but little use to them, and they have but a very small quantity of ammunition and are by no means expert in handling their newly acquired arms. These opinions are derived from the statements made by the very men who have been engaged in fighting them, and who have been magnified into heroes and warriors, with but very little reason.

Maj. Savage will probably remain with the commissioners for the purpose of acting as interpreter at the council fire. There is to be a grand feast given the chiefs; any number of beeves are to be roasted, innumerable pipes smoked, and a big talk held as soon as the red men come in, of all of which you should be apprized [sic] in due time.

The rain which commenced yesterday afternoon continued during the day, and last night at intervals, but fell in small quantities. The sun rose bright and clear this morning, but the sky has again become overcast, indicating more rain. The country is suffering dreadfully for it—the agricultural and mining interests being equally affected. The express is about starting, and so *adios.*

Executive Department
Sacramento City, April 8, 1852
To Gen. E. Hitchcock

Sir:

I have the honor to submit for your examination a letter addressed to me to-day by the Senators and Representatives from the Counties of Trinity, Klamath, Shasta and Siskiyou. You will learn, from a perusal of this communication, that there has been a resumption of hostilities in the North, and that our fellow citizens residing in the northern Counties are suffering the horrors of a predatory war. You are also presented with an aggregate statement of the number of citizens ruthlessly murdered in these counties by Savages within a "very few months" past. Annexed to this melancholy narrative is an aggregate statement of the value of property destroyed by Indians during the same period.

The history of these troubles, as recounted in this despatch [sic], and in other papers before me, show that the acts of these Savages are sometimes signalized by a ferocity worthy of the cannibals of the South Sea. They seem to cherish an instinctive hatred toward the white race, and this is a principle of their nature which neither time nor vicissitude can impair. This principle of hatred is hereditary, and it is transmitted from the live to the Son [life of the Son, meaning Jesus] by example and by injunction. Another infirmity of the Indian character of which we have incontestable evidence is that their respect for treaty stipulations ceases at the moment when the inciting causes—self interest or apprehensions of punishments—are removed. The character and conduct of these Indians presents an additional illustration of the accuracy of observations repeatedly made—that Whites and Indians cannot live in close proximity in peace; and it seems to confirm the opinion expressed in the enclosed despatch [sic] that an ultimate evacuation of the Northern Counties by Whites or the Indians will be unavoidable.

In contingencies like these a simple but imperative duty is imposed upon the Executive: to place the State in the hands of the General Government, and to demand from that aid and protection which the guaranties of the Federal Constitution assure us we are entitled to receive. If the General Government is neglectful of the demand which we make upon it—if it is unmindful of the duty which it owes to us—we have one other alternative—to fight our own battles—to maintain our independence as a sovereign but isolated State, and to protect ourselves from intestine troubles, as well as from the incursions of merciless and Savage enemies. Although we have found it necessary to embrace this alternative hitherto, we have not forgotten our allegiance to the

General Government, nor have I forgotten that devoted citizens, who respect their private and political obligations, possess the most sacred and binding claims upon the fostering protection of Government. The interests of a Government and a people are mutually dependent, and there is a line of reciprocal duty upon which a continuance of their mutual relations and interests depends. The citizen cannot absolve himself from this allegiance so long as he claims the protection of the Government, nor can the Government disregard the interests of the citizen in whatever quarter of the globe they may lie.

But, sir, it is my duty, however unpleasant it may be, to express conviction that adequate protection has not been extended by the Government in Washington to American citizens residing in the State of California. I refer particularly to the fact that the number of regular troops detailed for service in California and on the borders of Oregon, have not been proportionate to the demand of the service. The mountain Indians, whose activity, sagacity, and courage has never been surpassed by Indians on the continent of America, are untamed and unconquered. Collissons [sic] between them and American citizens have been frequent, and the number of victims sacrificed to this neglect of the General Government is being augmented every day. The strong and decisive interposition of that Government is now asked: if this reasonable petition is not granted, I am apprehensive that results will ensue which every true friend of the Government must deplore.

I deem it my duty to assure you that unless prompt protection is afforded to the citizens of this State by the General Government I shall feel constrained to resort to the only means left me to defend the frontiers and to conquer a lasting peace. A resort to these means will increase the debt of the State, and add to the burden of taxation imposed upon our citizens. To dispense with such necessity I indulge the earnest hope that you, as the military representative of the General Government in California will exercise your authority to arrest hostilities and to secure to us the blessings of a permanent peace.

In conclusion, permit me to suggest that if you have not at your immediate disposal a sufficient number of troops to detail for this service, and if you are authorized to state that the General Government will assume and pay expenses incident to a call of volunteers in to the Service, I will promptly issue a call for them whenever you may indicate a desire to have it done.

I have the honor to be, Sir, Your obt. servant

John Bigler

[Governor]

(National Archives, Records of the Department of War, Pacific Division, 1852, Letters Received, Box 4, Volume 2, Document C, as quoted in *The Destruction of California Indians*, pp. 188–91.)

Sacramento City, Cal.
To His Excellency
April 6, 1852
John Bigler, Governor of California

The undersigned Senators and Representatives from the Counties of Trinity, Klamath, Shasta, and Siskiyou, most respectfully represent to your Excellency that the constant and continued depredations committed by the various tribes of Indians on the lives and property of our citizens demand your prompt, efficient, and constant resistance that the citizens of this district are longer able to make, as a short review of the past history of the Section of our State and the present alarming situation of our citizens will demonstrate. Since the winter of 1848-50, the Pitt river Indians have been constantly hostile, and their incessant depredations and murders have been only occasionally checked by expeditions of the whites made into their country. All other tribes, to wit: the Cottonwood, Trinity, Klamath, and Shasta Indians, have, in turn, been hostile, and since the first settlement by the whites; but it has only been within the last few months that there appears to have been a general combination among them of hostility to the whites.

From our own personal knowledge, and from information obtained from reliable sources, we feel satisfied that the following statement of losses, both in life and property, that have occurred in our Section of the State from Indian depredations are considerably below the reality:

Shasta County

No. of whites murdered	40
Amount of property destroyed and stolen	$100,000

Trinity County

No. of whites murdered	20
Amount of property destroyed and stolen	$50,000

Klamath County

No. of whites murdered	50
Amount of property destroyed and stolen	$50,000

Siskiyou County

No. of whites murdered	20
Amount of property destroyed and stolen	$40,000

These enormous losses have all been sustained by the people of a small portion of this State, within a very few months. The evil is increasing every day as a more intimate knowledge of the whites makes the Indians more bold and reckless in their attacks. Already they enter our towns and villages at night and steal or set fire to property. The habitations of the industrious miners, while they are at their labors, are entered with impunity and robbed of their contents. The pack animals on which the miners must depend for their provisions, are either killed on the spot where found, or driven away to be roasted and eaten by the depredators. The people are compelled to travel from one portion of the country to another in companies, well armed to repel attacks.

It has been charged that the hostility of the Indians was superinduced by acts of injustice committed by the whites. As a general thing, we can state, from our own knowledge, that this has not been the case; and have no hesitation in saying that it emanates from the known character of the Indians— a mischievous disposition and desire for plunder. In but a few instances have the first offences [sic] been committed by the whites.

[Illegible] . . . order out the militia for that purpose. Eighty or one hundred men, in addition to those proposed to be located at Cow Creek, properly distributed in bands of ten to twenty, along Trinity and Klamath rivers, and always in readiness for service, would probably be sufficient; for the Indians now generally act in small parties, although, there has not often been much difficulty in repelling them yet, it has been almost impossible to follow them to their haunts to chastise them. Instances have occurred where miners have attempted this, and returned only to find their habitations despoiled of every thing valuable.

For these reasons, we now ask of you protection for the people of that portion of the State that has never yet received any thing at the hands of the Government, confidently expecting your speedy attention to the same.

We remain very Respectfully,
Your obt. Servants
Signed Thomas H. Coats of Klamath County,
Samuel Fleming, E. D. Pierce of Shasta County,
Geo. O. McMullin of Trinity County,
J. W. Denver, Senator from Klamath & Trinity Counties,
R. J. Sprague, Senator from Shasta.

(National Archives, Records of the Department of War, Pacific Division, 1852, Letters Received, Box 4, Volume 2, Document C, as quoted in *The Destruction of California Indians*, pp. 191–93.)

Daily Alta California, March 31, 1853

Indian disturbances have begun again in the Northern and Southern portions of the State. The principal feature of the tidings this morning from Los Angeles is the threatening state of Indian affairs. A statement appears to the Los Angeles paper prepared by D. WILSON, Indian Agent for that district, in which he advises the organization of volunteer companies to go against the tribes who cause the chief annoyance to the people of Los Angeles and vicinity; and urges that they may be whipped into subjection and taught to respect American laws by a timely, vigorous and determined step of this kind. Mr. Wilson is probably better acquainted with the habits and disposition of those Indians than any other American residing in the South, and his counsel is not without its weight. In former times, during the reign of the Spanish law, the rancheros could only compel obedience to their government by such a course as that which Mr. Wilson proposes. There is danger, however, that volunteer companies, not under sufficient restraint to check the propensity to profit by an advantage, may be guilty of indiscretions and excesses in the destruction of human life and appropriation of property among the Indians, that will not be altogether creditable to the State, nor agreeable to the feelings of the Indian Agent.

Daily Alta California, April 19, 1853

The tenacity which some people have manifested in their efforts to effect a reduction in the wages of labor and to lower and degrade it by bringing into competition with free white labor that of inferior races is marvelous. It has been attempted at various times to introduce negro [sic], Asiatic, Kanaka and every other kind of labor that could be had at a cheaper rate than can that of American citizens. The last thing we have heard of in this line appears in the form of a bill introduced in the Assembly yesterday, the purport of which was to reduce the Indians to a state of slavery. The bill is very long and provides to have the Indians bound out for any given number of years to serve such white men as will give the required security for their maintenance and support. There are various provisions and penalties in the bill, but they do not hide the fact that the effect of its passage will be to render the miserable and degraded remnant of a happy race, which is fast fading from the face of the earth, the servants and dependents of their exterminators. An act of this kind will surely sound badly in history. The Indians! the poor degenerate Indians! Is it not enough that they are fast fading away and that all that remains of a race that once peopled this entire land are now too low and degraded to resist, and is it possible that the closing act of the fading drama of the red man's history is to be the reducing him to a state to which an Indian never submitted before. It is true they may be placed in a better condition physically than if they roam wild as has been their way. But so it suits them, and no other life can now render them any happier, and we trust that all attempts to render them subjects of their superiors will at once be indignantly voted down.

Amendments in 1860 to the Act of April 1850

Chap. CCXXXI—An Act amendatory of an Act entitled, "An Act for the Government and Protection of Indians," passed April twenty-second, one thousand eight hundred and fifty. [Approved April 18, 1860.]

The People of the State of California, represented in Senate and Assembly, do enact as follows:

SECTION 1. Section third of said act, is hereby amended so as to read as follows:

SEC. 3. County and District Judges in the respective counties of this State, shall, by virtue of this act, have full power and authority, at the instance and request of any person having or hereafter obtaining any Indian child or children, male or female, under the age of fifteen years, from the parents or person or persons having the care or charge of such child or children, with the consent of such parents or person or persons having the care or charge of any such child or children, or at the instance and request of any person desirous of obtaining any Indian or Indians, whether children or grown persons, that may be held as prisoners of war, or at the instance and request of any person desirous of obtaining any vagrant Indian or Indians, as have no settled habitation or means of livelihood, and have not placed themselves under the protection of any white person, to bind and put out such Indians as apprentices, to trades, husbandry, or other employments, as shall to them appear proper, and for this purpose shall execute duplicate articles of indenture of apprenticeship on behalf of such Indians, which indentures shall also be executed by the person to whom such Indian or Indians are to be indentured; one copy of which shall be filed by the County Judge, in the Recorder's office of the county, and one copy retained by the person to whom such Indian or Indians may be indentured; such indentures shall authorize such person to have the care, custody, control, and earnings, of such Indian or Indians, as shall require such person to clothe and suitably provide the necessaries of life for such Indian or Indians, for and during the term for which such Indian or Indians, shall be apprenticed, and shall contain the sex, name, and probable age, of such Indian or Indians; such indentures may be for the following terms of years: Such children as are under fourteen years of age, if males, until they attain the age of twenty-five years; if females, until they attain the age of twenty-one years; such as are over fourteen and under twenty years, then next following the date of such indentures, for and during the term of ten years, at the discretion of such Judge; such Indians as may be indentured under the provision of this section, shall be deemed within such provisions of this act, as are applicable to minor Indians.

SEC. 2. Section seventh of said act is hereby amended so as to read as follows:

SEC. 7. If any person shall forcibly convey any Indian from any place without this State, to any place within this State, or from his or her home within this State, or compel him or her to work or perform any service, against his or her will, except as provided in this act, he or they shall, upon conviction thereof, be fined in any sum not less than one hundred dollars, nor more than five hundred dollars, before any court having jurisdiction at the discretion of the court, and the collection of such fine shall be enforced as provided by law in other criminal cases, one-half to be paid to the prosecutor, and one-half to the county in which such conviction is had.

(Chapter 231 of *Statutes of California*, enacted into law on April 18, 1860.)

Daily Alta California, November 13, 1851

Murder in Santa Barbara.—An Indian was murdered in Santa Barbara, recently, under circumstances which call loudly for the establishment of a Vigilance Committee in that place. He was called from the house by a Sonorian, whose name we did not learn, and who without any provocation whatever, plunged a knife into his heart, killing him instantly. Some four or five Indians were present, witnesses to the transaction, and they pursued the murderer, caught him and carried him before a magistrate. Will it be believed that he was almost immediately released from custody, because our laws will not allow an Indian to testify against a white man.

Daily Alta California, January 5, 1853

SAN FRANCISCO, Jan. 4th, 1853

GENTLEMEN: In your report to the *Alta* of this morning, of the decision of the United States Land Commissioners, in the case of A. A. Ritherie, claiming the rancho of Suisun, you state the "objection was taken, in the ground of the blood of the grantee, he being an Indian," which was not considered satisfactory to the Commissioners, "inasmuch as the Mexican constitution, laws and decrees fully recognized persons of that race as citizens of the Republic, and entitled to all consideration as such."

Now, as any objection to the grant could only have proceeded from me, as the only law agent of the United States present, and the only person heard in objection to the claim, it concerns me materially, that my objection should be correctly stated, and that I should not be represented, as I am in this report, maintaining a proposition, utterly untenable and unfounded.

My argument, which was entirely wanting, and is now before me, was, on the contrary, in a great measure devoted to the establishment of the fact of the entire abolition, by the Mexican government, of all distinctions founded on blood or race or descent alone; and consequently, of the entire equality of all Mexicans, according to the legal definition of the term Mexicans, whether of Indian, African, European or any other race.

No objection whatever was urged by me against the grant to Solano, or against the transfer of the property by him to Vallejo, on the ground that he was of Indian blood; my objection, and the only one urged by me, was founded on the fact as declared by him in his petition to Vallejo for permission to occupy the land, and as declared, moreover, in the grant of property to him by Governor Alvarado, that he was a savage Indian and the chief of a tribe of savage Indians, and that as such he was not a Mexican, nor entitled to receive a grant of lands in California, which by laws of Mexico could only be made to Mexicans.

This was the objection made by me to the grant, and it must have been the same, not considered satisfactory by Commissioner Thornton, as no other was made on the trial. Whether I established it or not, or what arguments I used, are questions which I do not propose to examine: my only object being to relieve myself from the imputetion [sic] of endeavoring to sustain a proposition so utterly contrary to all well known facts, as that any one could be disqualified by the Mexican Constitution or laws, from holding or disposing lands, or from exercising any other rights on account of his blood or race, or descent alone, without any other grounds of disqualification.

I am, sir, very respectfully, your obedient servant,
ROBERT GREENHOW,
Associate Law Agent of the U.S.

SUGGESTED READING

Carrico, Richard L. *Strangers in a Stolen Land*. Newcastle, Calif.: Sierra Oaks
  Publishing, 1987.
Castillo, Edward, and Robert Jackson. *Indians, Franciscans, and Spanish
  Colonization*. Albuquerque: University of New Mexico Press, 1995.
Heizer, Robert F., ed. *The Destruction of California Indians*. Santa Barbara,
  Calif.: Peregrine Smith, 1974.
Heizer, Robert F., and Alan J. Almquist. *The Other Californians*. Berkeley:
  University of California Press, 1971.
Hurtado, Albert. *Indian Survival on the California Frontier*. New Haven,
  Conn.: Yale University Press, 1988.
Jackson, Donald Dale. *Gold Dust*. New York: Alfred A. Knopf, 1980.
Phillips, George H. *Chiefs and Challengers: Indian Resistance and
  Cooperation in Southern California*. Berkeley: University of California
  Press, 1975.
———. *The Enduring Struggle*. San Francisco: Boyd & Fraser Publishing
  Company, 1981.
———. *Indians and Indian Agents*. Norman: University of Oklahoma Press,
  1997.
———. *Indians and Intruders in Central California, 1769–1849*. Norman:
  University of Oklahoma Press, 1993.
Rawls, James J. "Gold Diggers: Indian Miners in the California Gold Rush."
  California Historical Quarterly 60 (1976): 28–45.
———. *Indians of California*. Norman: University of Oklahoma Press, 1984.
Rohrbough, Malcolm J. *Days of Gold*. Berkeley: University of California
  Press, 1997.

Spicer, Edward H. *Cycles of Conquest.* Tucson: University of Arizona Press, 1962.

Trafzer, Clifford E. *California's Indians and the Gold Rush.* Newcastle, Calif.: Sierra Oaks Publishing Company, 1989.

Wagner, Henry R. *Juan Rodriguez Cabrillo, Discoverer of the Coast of California.* San Francisco: California Historical Society, 1941.

Weber, David J. *The Mexican Frontier, 1821–46.* Albuqerque: University of New Mexico Press, 1982.

———. *The Spanish Frontier in North America.* New Haven, Conn.: Yale University Press, 1992.

INDEX

murder(s): *Daily Alta California* on, 39, 40,
43–49, 51; of California Natives, 2–3, 7,
10, 17–18, 24, 28–29, 68; attributed to
Natives, 25–26, 39, 43–45, 48, 76, 96,
154; hangings, 76, 77, 96, 97, 120, 122;
by the military, 28; and Santa Barbara
vigilantes, 158; whites began the
Native, 2; white's outrageous, 51,
129–30; of women and children, 18, 29,
68, 76, 115, 124–25, 129, 130, 131–32.
See also California Native Americans;
extermination; massacres; Morehead;
newspapers; racism; Savage, James
Murphy, Mr., (legislator), 145
Myles, H. R., 87

Naglee, Henry, 13–14
Nailon, John, 122
Napa, California, 78
Native American (Peoples): Apache, 93;
Arizona, 56; Cherokee, x , 3, 17; Utah,
56, 64; Ute, 12; Wyandot, 3, 17; Yuma,
58, 60, 61, 62. *See also* California Native
American Peoples; California Native
Americans
Necate, Francis, 110
Nevada County, California, 53
Nevada National, 53
New Helvetia, 13. *See also* Sutter, John
Augustus
New Mexico, 12
newspapers: on California natural history,
46–47; on extermination policy, 47–48,
50, 113–33; Garra Revolt in the, 81, 95,
97, 99, 103, 104, 108–12; honesty in the,
23; Manifest Destiny in, 41–42, 48, 49,
55, 65–66; murder articles in, 39, 40, 43,
49–51, 113–33; negative or biased
images of Natives in the, 25–26, 27,
35–53; Native culture presented in, 45,
46, 53; Native resistance raid articles in,
56–70, 71–79; Natives' viewpoint in the,
35–36, 49, 51–52; presented views on
the holocaust, xiv. *See also Red Bluff
Beacon; San Francisco Evening Bulletin;
California Farmer; Century; Chico
Courant; Shasta Courier; Tuolumne
Courier; Daily Alta California; Gazette;*

*San Francisco Daily Herald; Humboldt
Times; Nevada County Journal;
Marysville Appeal; Monterey
Californian; Nevada National; News;
Shasta Republican; Sacramento Union;
San Joaquin Republican; San Jose Argus;
Sonora Democrat; Los Angeles Star; Los
Angeles Times; San Francisco Placer
Times and Transcript; San Diego Union*
New York Volunteers, 37, 43, 61. *See also*
Stevenson, John
"Nigger", 2, 35
Nimekaw People, 120
Nipaguay village, 9
Nissenan People: built Sutter's Mill, 1, 15;
Sutter's treaty and, ix
Nome Lackee Reservation, 27
Northern Mines. *See* American River; Deer
Creek; Feather River; Humboldt;
Klamath River; Marysville; Placerville;
Sacramento River; Shasta; Trinity
County
North Yager Creek, 79
Norton, Jack, xiv
Norton, M. (Major), 108
Norton, Mr., 48
Numtarimon (chief), 45

Oak Grove, 68
Odeneil. *See* O'Donnell, William
O'Donnell, Peter, 83–84
O'Donnell, William, 83, 84, 90
Ohio (ship), 93, 99
Oklahoma, 14
"Old Uncle Ned", 46
Oliviera, Augustin, 87
Oregon: miners attacked by Natives, 36;
miners as murderers, 17, 36; newspaper
articles on the Indian war in, 49; as
rapists, 2, 17; troops in, 143
Orleans Bar, California, 132
Ortega, Mr., 111
Osburn, W. B., 87, 89
Other Californians, The (Heizer and
Almquist), xv, 125
Owen, Dick, 24, 66, 67
Owen's Lake, 116
Owens Valley, 29